BLACK COUNTRY ROOTS

Black Country lives told in the words of Black Country people

Canal fishing, Oxley, 1980.
Photo: Dave Bagnall

Preface

This book is about the African-Caribbean communities of the Black Country, told in the words of the people themselves.

The stories are about the journeys people made in order to answer the call from Britain to help rebuild after the war. They are also about the everyday struggles of making a new home in a strange place whilst trying to find work and bring up a family.

There are stories of the terrible racism encountered and the resilience that it took to carry on.

These experiences are all the more important to remember in light of the resistance to the new immigration to the UK being experienced today.

The book is illustrated with photography from local archives but also from the work of photographers who have been fascinated with uncovering the extraordinary life of Black Country people over the years.

Thank you to all of the people who shared their stories and personal photographs for this book.

Emma Chetcuti, Director, Multistory

Interviewed contributors

Richard Bair
Alison Brown
Don Campbell
Lauren Campbell
Errol Drummond
Mavis Edwards-Stewart
Jeremy Grant
Justice Holtec
Kenneth James
Hyacinth Jarrett
Mr Johns
Avtar Singh Jouhl
Anthony McFarlane
Joyce Nelson
Lawrence Nelson
Marva Nisbett
Akinwande Phillips
John Siffa
Annette Simms
Stanley Simms
Jackie Taylor
Malachi Thomas
Miss U (Eugenie Samuels)
Shane Ward
Serbert Williams
Rose Wilkins
Oniel Wright

Introduction

I am so proud to be introducing this book. I asked Emma Chetcuti of Multistory if they would help us produce a book about the African-Caribbean community of the Black Country. I knew that there was a great story to tell, of the challenges, the happiness and the determination of the African-Caribbean people who came to the Black Country.

I hope this book will be a tribute to all of the black people of the Black Country and will help the younger generation discover what their parents and grandparents went through to become a part of the community.

Cllr Jackie Taylor
The first African-Caribbean elected councillor in Sandwell.

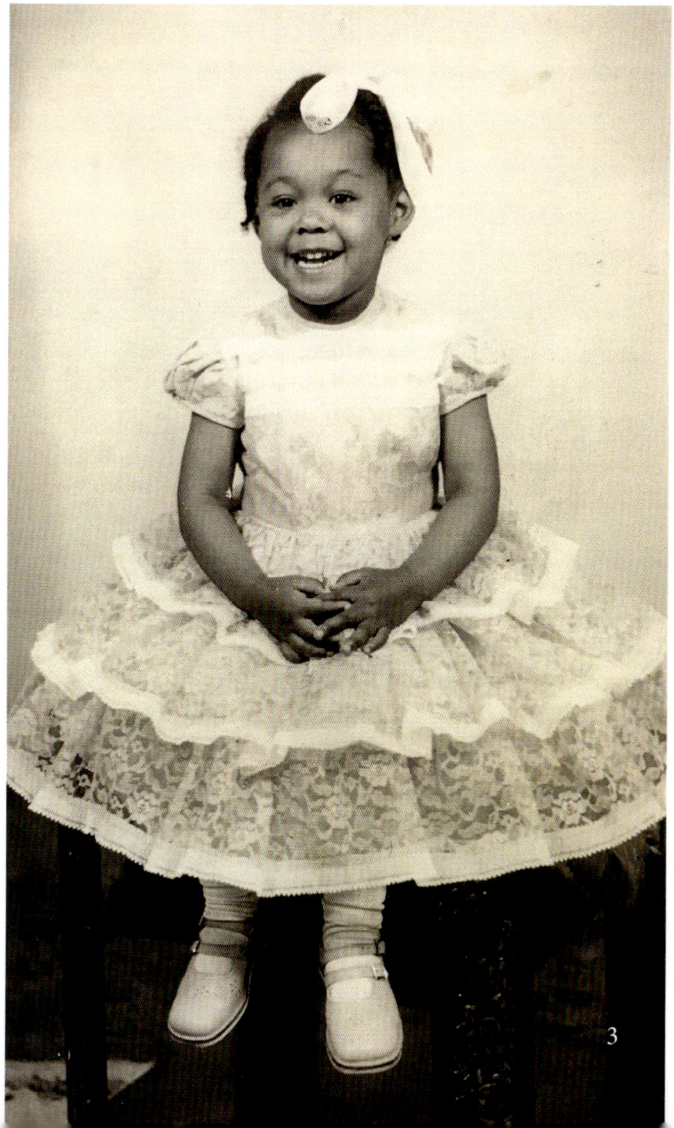

Cllr Jackie Taylor as a young girl

350 years ago there were black people living in the Black Country and the West Midlands

People have always travelled. Even hundreds of years ago black people were living in the Black Country and the West Midlands and there were white people living in places like the Caribbean islands. Annette Simms has a recollection of this in her own family.

My grandma was married to an Irish guy because, in slavery times, Jamaica was a different place. In those times there were all different nations, all different countries going there.
Annette Simms

Date	Location	Detail
1662	Llanforda	Samson, 'Negro' Gardener on estate in Oswestry, Shropshire
1663	Evesham	Martha, a 'Neger' was baptised and buried at All Saints Church
1667	Chaddesley Corbett	Burial of a 'son of an Egyptian'
1668	Ashley	Laurence, an 'African of the Christian faith' was buried at St John's
1675	Barlaston	Peter Blackman, a 'blackamore' was baptised at St John's
1676	Wolstanton	John Mills, Black churchwarden of parish church
1680	Charlecote	Black page depicted in painting of Captain Lucy
1687	Driffield	George Hanger, baptised in June
1690	Idlicote	Jan 1st, baptism of Margaret Lucy, 'negro slave to Lady Underhill'
1698	Lenchwick	John Langley, 30, a 'Niger of Jameca' baptised 6th January
1700	Oxhill	Will Archus, adult Black male, baptised
1704	Bishops Castle	Black page boy (aged 10) to Charles Mason, MP
1704	Birtsmorton	Susanna, 'negro' servant to Countess of Bellomont was baptised
1705	Oxhill	Myrtilla, 'negro slave to Thos Beauchamp', buried
1705	Tipton	John, 'Ethyopian page to Lady Pye' baptised
1712	Ilmington	Frances Warrington, escaped slave from Constantinople, baptised
1713	Worcester	Peter Kuffey, 'a Black, Ellison's servant', baptism at St John's
1716	Ombersley	John Morgan, 'son of a Jamaican' was baptised
1725	Broadway	Harry Worcester, 7 year old Black servant to Edward Popham baptised
1726	Twyning	Thomas Gloucester, Black servant of Ambrose Baldwynn was baptised
1735	Charlecote	Phillip Lucy, 6 year old Black slave was baptised
1741	Tamworth	A Black 'drummers child' was buried
1749	Birmingham	Black Slave working as furnaceman for Lloyd family, (p. 8)
1752	Sheinton	Cato and Anthony, West Indians were baptised
1755	Grandborough	Lewis, Black servant to Mr. Rodburn was baptised
1756	Alcester	Pulford Power, 14 year old 'negro' was baptised
1757	Lenchwick	Anthony Camdaye, 'negro' servant to Mr Brown of Charlston was baptised
1762	Culworth	Charles Bacchus, African servant, buried St Mary's church
1765	Stafford	Three Black drummers with 38th Foot regiment
1766	Shifnal	Benjamin Prioleu, 'black' servant to Mr Austin of Aston was baptised
1766	Wolverhampton	George Africanus, Black servant to Molineux family, baptised (p.12)
1768	Shifnal	Charleston, 'negro' servant to Walter Mansell was baptised
1771	Wolverhampton	Richard Crosby Africanus, 'adult negro' was baptised
1771	Kidderminster	Ukawsaw Gronniosaw, ex-slave, lived here with his family (p. 14)
1771	Lichfield	Sale by auction, 'creole slave, 21, speaks good English, good with horses'
1771	Lichfield	Sale by auction at the Bakers Arms, 'negro slave, aged ten or eleven'
1773	Kingsland	Black servant baptised, (Herefordshire)

Right: A list of early black inhabitants of the West Midlands from 'History Detectives, Black people in the West Midlands 1650 – 1918' by Barbara Willis-Brown and David Callaghan. Courtesy of SCAWDI

Above: William Davidson, born 1780s, a black cabinet-maker who worked and lived in Staffordshire.
Top: thought to be of Francis Barber, 1742 – 1801, Lichfield & Birmingham, reputedly painted by James Northcote. Courtesy of the Trustees of Dr Johnson's House
Right: Thomas Richards, born 1872, probably the first photograph of a black person in West Bromwich.
Photo: Staffordshire Record Office

My dad worked on tobacco farms before he came to Birmingham

My dad had travelled as a younger man before coming to England, and worked in Connecticut in America. He actually worked on tobacco farms, that kind of work. It was very much like chopping cane really. Hard work that my dad enjoyed but he used to reap the rewards of that as well.
Cllr Jackie Taylor

Above: Two men cut Burley tobacco on Russell Spears' farm in Lexington County, Kentucky. September, 1940. Library of Congress Commons: No known restrictions on publication.
Right: Workers in the field gathering tobacco leaves, Special Collections Research Centre, North Carolina State University Libraries. Tobacco (UA023.034.041)

We were invited to help rebuild the motherland

Slum clearance, Ladywood about 1965. Photo: Peter Donnelly

Helping rebuild the Motherland

Somebody, High Commissioner or whatever, some Department of Works guy came over to the Caribbean, set up in the town centre and just recruited people to come and work. No specific jobs. I think the mantra was to 'help rebuild the Motherland'.
Then we had an influx of Barbadians, mainly bus drivers. The Caribbeans came and a lot of them came to the Midlands, to Birmingham actually, and they worked in the factories, on the buses. My uncle was on the buses. My dad worked in a factory for a very short time. Never liked it.
Errol Drummond

According to my mum she just filled out an application and came. My dad did exactly the same thing.
Anthony McFarlane

I was born in Jamaica, came here in 1955. I came by boat. Santa Maria I think it was.
Joyce Nelson

Right: Windrush children arriving, photographer unknown.
Opposite page: The Empire Windrush, June, 1948.
Photo: Getty Images

EMPIRE WINDRUSH
LONDON

We didn't come on a banana boat, we was requested to come!

When they came here they were told the whole 'Windrush story' that there'd be loads of work and loads of jobs. People were literally saying it's called the Windrush because we're rushing to get over here.
Justice Holtec

What happened in those days, the men would immigrate first, obviously looking for work. In fact, they were recruited to come to the UK to help rebuild.
Errol Drummond

I ended up working in factories and in those days it was easy to get work.

I could just walk from one job to another. If I don't want one, I just left it and go somewhere else. But the factory work was heavy. I decided to make the most of it and, if I didn't settle down, then I would just go back. I was missing everybody and I'm thinking, 'I need to send money home so I really can't go back, I need to work to send money home'.

Then I met my husband, got married and started a family and, although I'd got children I was still working. He'd go out during the day, came in, and I'm going out, so it was like passing by.
Annette Simms

Us immigrants, we made a contribution to England. I was contributing before Cameron and Farage was born! We didn't come on a banana boat, we was requested to come! We were given the impression we would be respected, looked after, but that didn't happen. You've got to have politicians to run the country for all - not just for the few. We've been chucked against the fence.
Malachi Thomas

I was born in Trinidad. I wasn't one of the invited ones. I came because of a desire to come. But when I came nobody said hello. I used to walk about the streets until the cocks went crowing, alone.
Marva Nisbett

A trio of Jamaican immigrants walking the streets of Birmingham. 22 January, 1955. Photo: Thurston Hopkins / Picture Post / Getty Images

A lot of our people from Caribbean come over and fight here in the war

So we had a lot of Caribbean people come across to support Britain in different ways, right? Whether it's on the battlefield, in the NHS, in industry.
Don Campbell

My dad left Jamaica to come and fight in the war. A lot of our people from Jamaica come over and fight here in the war, and sometimes they don't get acknowledged that they did that.
Annette Simms

My granddad, he was in British Rail. He worked for them for his whole life and he started off doing all sorts of stuff and built his way up to the point where he had a really good, high-paid job. It's almost like, you think about the railway stations and the fact that travel is so important, it shows you how important we have been in contributing to help build the travel system.
Justice Holtec

Marva Nisbett
Photo from Marva Nisbett

Flt. Sgt. Victor Emmanuel Tucker
Photo: © Imperial War Museums
(CH 5312)

This is cold, man, this is cold!

When I landed, all I could see was this white stuff and I thought, 'What's that down there?' Then come my dad and he said, 'It's snow' and I'm thinking, 'This is cold, man, this is cold, I don't know if I can stay here; it is cold!' When I look at the houses and see smoke coming out a chimney it looks like the house was caught on fire.

It was just change, because I'm leaving a hot country and coming to somewhere cold and it looked different, and I'm thinking, 'Will I be all right? I may have to end up going back'.
Annette Simms

It was very cold. It was cold in that October. The snow would be on the ground for weeks and it would be very thick snow. It's not thin, it's layered. And then the frost comes and it becomes ice. So falling down and hurting yourself was quite regular.

The council used to have to send the council workers around to actually shovel the ice and put it on lorries to move it. That was how bad it was.
Hyacinth Jarrett

Because it was a cold country, in the winter they used to get some bad fogs because the houses was belching out smoke and so were the trains and the factories. That caused a lot of problems.

I remember right on the High Street, here in West Bromwich, I've seen it with my own eyes, when the fog came down, the buses couldn't run. There was a man who had to walk in front to lead the bus to take people to work. If I put my hand out in front of me, I couldn't see my own hand with that thick fog that come down. It used to hurt people, some people died from it.
Stanley Simms

I'd never seen snow before so I asked my mother what it was and she told me it was snow. I didn't even understand that word because we never used it, and I didn't try to find out where it was from. You know, a silly question, maybe, but I just didn't. It wasn't snowing at the time, it was just on the ground. So I didn't know it had come out of the sky.
Don Campbell

The Black Country, 1960s
Photo: John Bulmer

The only place in Jamaica that had bricks was the prison

The first thing that hit me was the bricks on the houses because the only place in Jamaica that had bricks was the prison!
Hyacinth Jarrett

When I arrived in a taxi I looked up and all I could see was like smoke coming up through the roof chimney, 'I'm not coming out!' I says, 'I didn't say I'm going to a factory'. The taxi driver says, 'This is where you are going'. So I says, 'No, I'm not coming out'. I'd seen smoke, we'd got nothing like that in Jamaica unless it was a fire. No! This cannot be a house. This has got to be a factory.

Well, these two men come out, it was two brothers. They took me in and I had a warm welcome there. A very, very warm welcome from both.
Miss U

I landed on the 20th July, which was a Sunday, and I was collected from Heathrow and driven to Birmingham. Like most people from the Caribbean the first impression was the houses being close together, it's not something that we are used to. Normally the houses are spread. Your neighbour is probably, if you're lucky, within shouting distance but normally quite a way away. Seeing houses joined together, it took me several days to figure out that I cannot get to next door's, because next door is somebody else's house!

Something that stands out as well was a long summer evening, if you like. In the Caribbean, it get to dusk round about five, five thirty, and it's pitch black by six o'clock, six thirty and, you know, here, I'm a young lad, at seven thirty and it was very bright outside; the sun was shining. Eight o'clock, the sun was shining, nine o'clock the sun was shining. It was almost ten o'clock and it was still bright. And I'm sitting here thinking, 'Well something's definitely wrong, but has anybody else noticed?'
Errol Drummond

Cherry Orchard, Old Hill, 1966. Photo: Sandwell Community History & Archive Service (CHAS)

I'm a human being as well, I don't get it

I knock on the door, to see if I could get a room. And some of them just shut the door in your face. And some of them said, 'No dogs allowed'. That was for us, as black people. So what's happening now to the immigrants coming to this country is what they done to us.
Mavis Edwards-Stewart

You couldn't get anywhere to live. They used to put in the windows 'No blacks, no Irish, no dogs'. So there were three black owners who had houses, and every black person who come here actually head for those houses because there was nowhere else for you to go.
Hyacinth Jarrett

When it happened at the time you're thinking, 'I don't get it. They're a human being, I'm a human being as well, so why are you treating each other in that way?'
Annette Simms

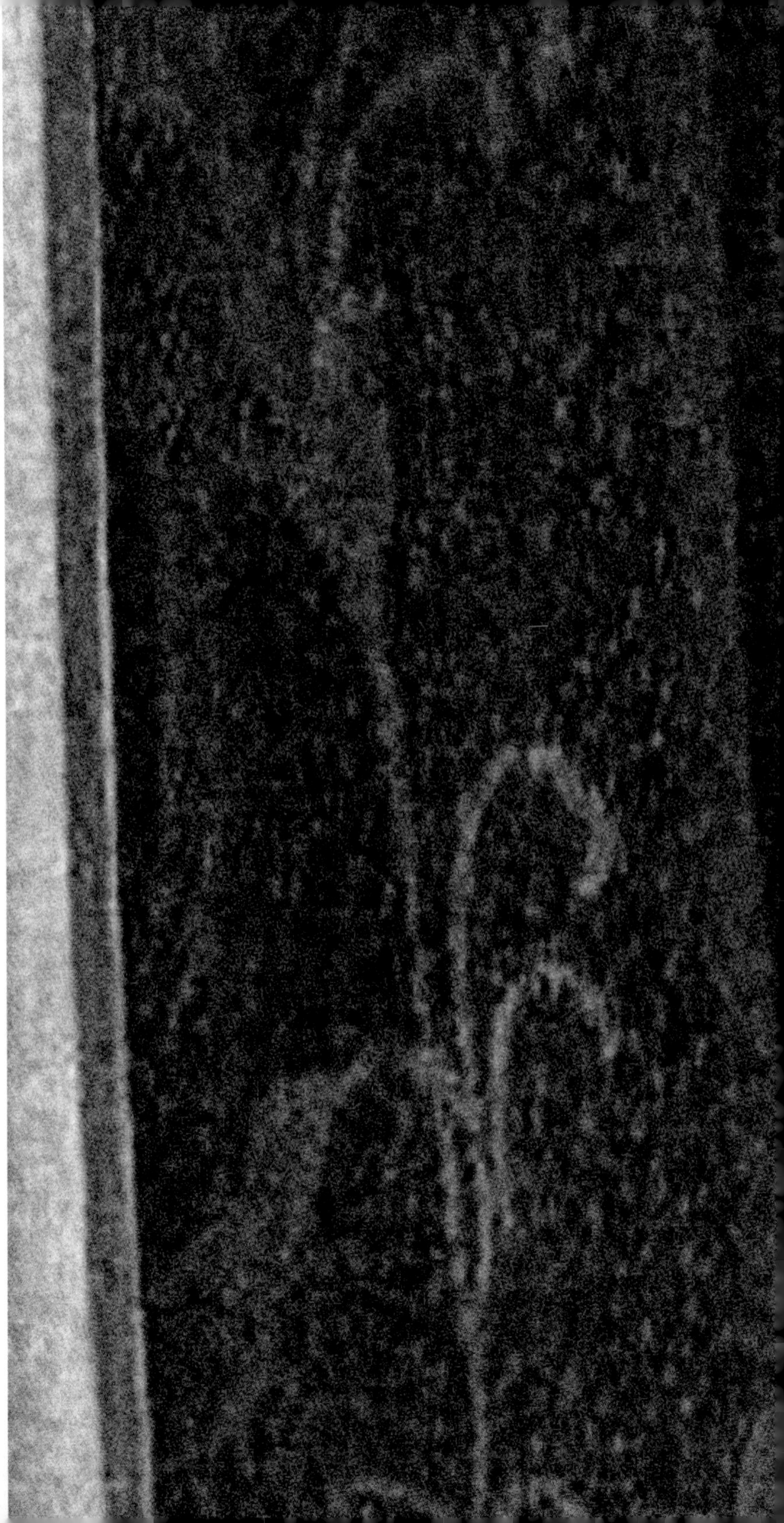

Window sign, Smethwick, 1965.
Photographer unknown.

ROOM TO RENT
NO BLACKS
NO IRISH

They just ignore you like you're not there

I'd walk in the road and I'd get these funny remarks and sometimes they'd just come out with some words and I'm thinking, 'Why did they say that to me?'

Then again, it's not everybody was like that. Most of the time people were quite nice and you sort of get used to those people that are nice to you and those that are not.

Then I would end up going to the shop to buy clothes and stuff and they just ignore you like you're not there. I go to the pub and they just walk past you and go to somebody else.

Then I complain to the person that would manage it and I'd say, 'He's ignoring me'. We'd go to the restaurant, they walk past your table and they go on to someone else and you're there before they were.

It was like why are they doing what they're doing? But long before I came, other people were going through the same thing or perhaps worse than I was. Black, white, Irish, everybody perhaps, was going through the same from people because you look different and you talk different. It's like, 'What are you doing here?'

Annette Simms

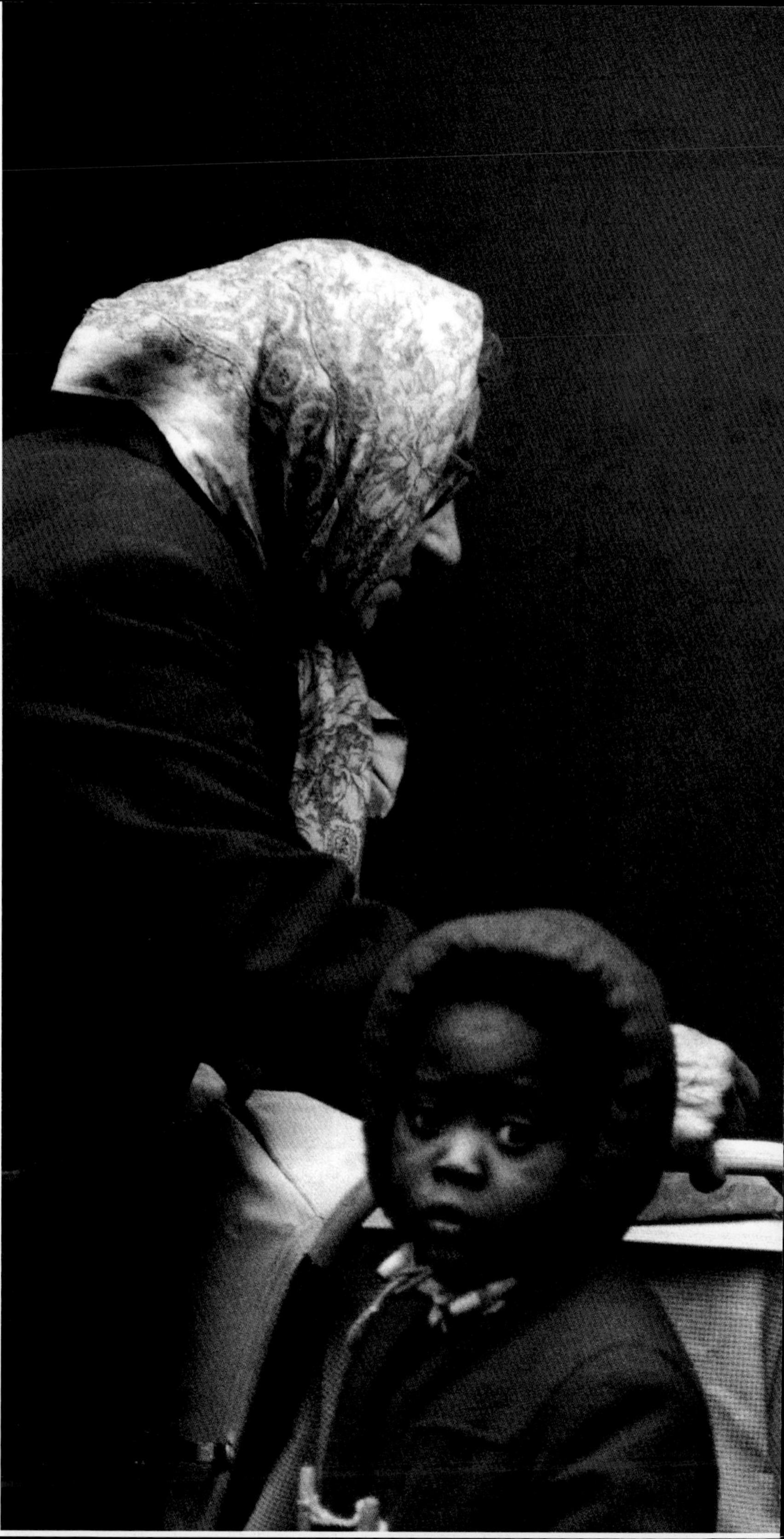

The Black Country, 1960s
Photos: John Bulmer

I can start on Monday

We worked in the factories, on the buses

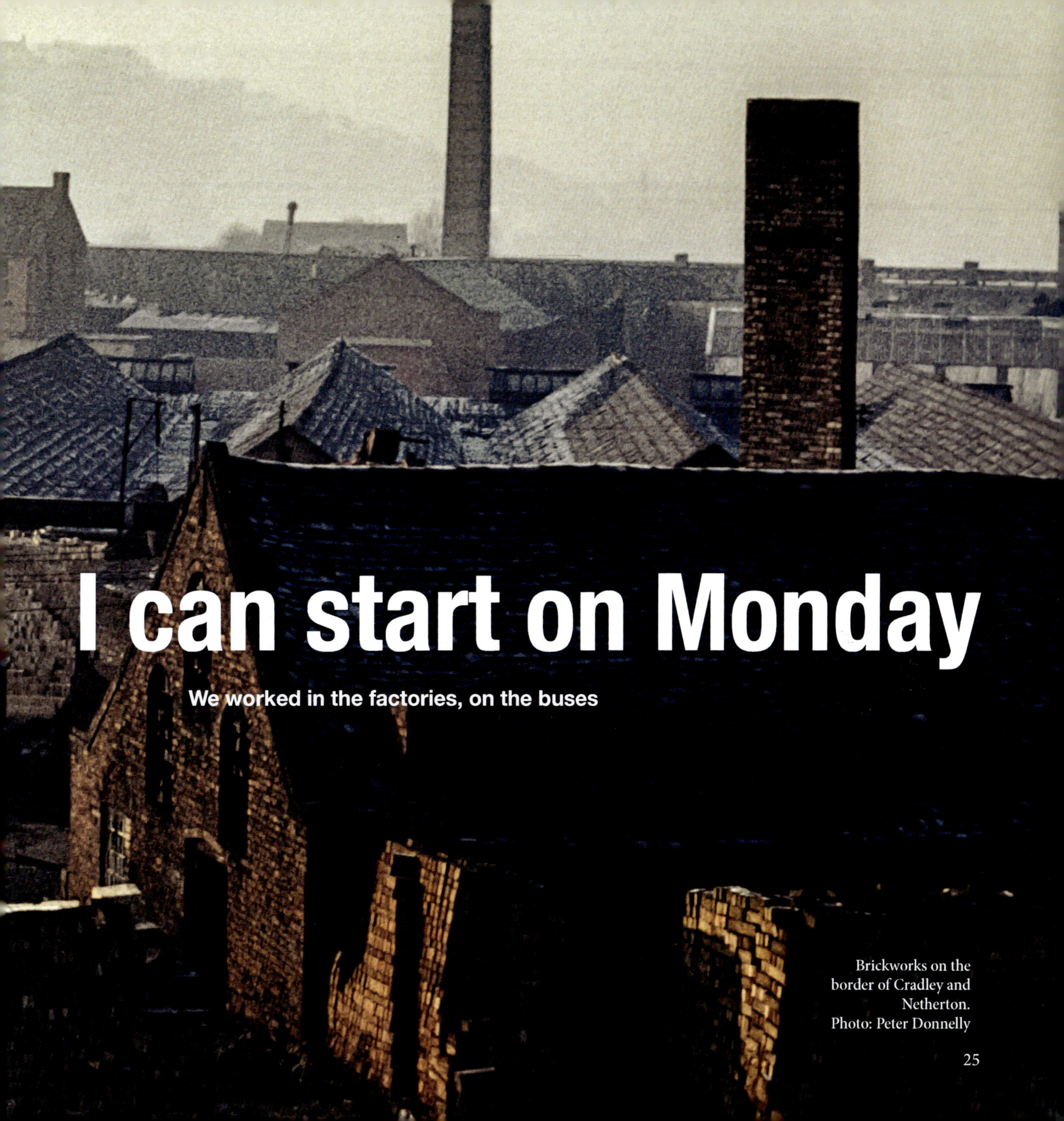

Brickworks on the border of Cradley and Netherton.
Photo: Peter Donnelly

In those days it was easy to get work in the Black Country but the factory work was heavy and dangerous

People got killed, because it was a really dangerous job.

The one night there was an explosion. There was a big acid plant, some giant tanks about a hundred feet high each, and I usually walked past about half past four when I finish to walk out of the factory. I got home here, I was watching the 6 o'clock news and they said there was an explosion at the company, the tank was blown apart. If it was earlier, I would have got killed.

It was dangerous because we used to make material that goes into bombs and sometimes it used to be about 90 degrees when you are working. You have to make sure you are not sweating because if your sweat fall into the material that you are making, a drop of water, it would explode. It was dangerous work.
Kenneth James

Right:
Making tea in an enamel jug, blast furnace cabin, Bilston, 1976.
Photo: Nick Hedges

Opposite page:
Hand rolling steel billets, Birchley Rolling Mills, Oldbury, 1976.
Photo: Nick Hedges

All I know is, I'm dead

I remember this guy was loading the wagons to go in the furnace and the button was pressed to pull the wagons in and he got trapped between the wagons - you know - when they stopped it. They asked him if he was alright and he said, 'All I know is, I'm dead'. That was his reply - and he was dead.

Another good friend, he was changing the carbon on the furnace and the cable cut, and chopped his arm off.
Kenneth James

My parents said, 'Don't work in a factory if you can help it because it's not very good and you wont enjoy it. But go and experience it if you don't believe us. And then go and do the thing that you really want to do'.
Anthony McFarlane

They had no health and safety in hospitals and factories in those days.
Hyacinth Jarrett

Left: Frontside steel furnace man, British Steel, Bilston, 1976. Photo: Nick Hedges

Right: Steelworker's hand, 1976. Photo: Nick Hedges

In those days, in the West Bromwich Corporation, they value you as a person

In 1968, I think it was November, I passed my bus driving test. I was the youngest bus driver, 21 years old.

At first I was with the Corporation; it was lovely working for them. In the summer you go out with the mayor, like a beach trip, sometimes to Blackpool but every driver and conductor can't go at the same time. So from about the end of May and the beginning of June up to August every weekend there is a certain group, so much goes then with the mayor until everybody gets their turn. The other time, to Morecambe, I went there. The mayor always comes with us.

It was happy until National Express took over; it's not as happy as what it used to be. In those days in the West Bromwich Corporation they value you as a person. Nowadays you're just a number.

Then they made one man buses. No conductor. They come up with a new idea that they put a machine at the side, so you can self service. Drop your money in the machine but that machine it come up with a copy of the money what you put in. If you put a penny in it come out with a picture of the penny. So any money you drop in you can't say you put in this, it prints it on the ticket.

My favourite route was the 92 to Wolverhampton. When I get to Wolverhampton sometimes we have 20 minutes and at the time we could leave the bus and walk about in the town. Then we head over to Streetly, in the countryside, that was lovely too.
Serbert Williams

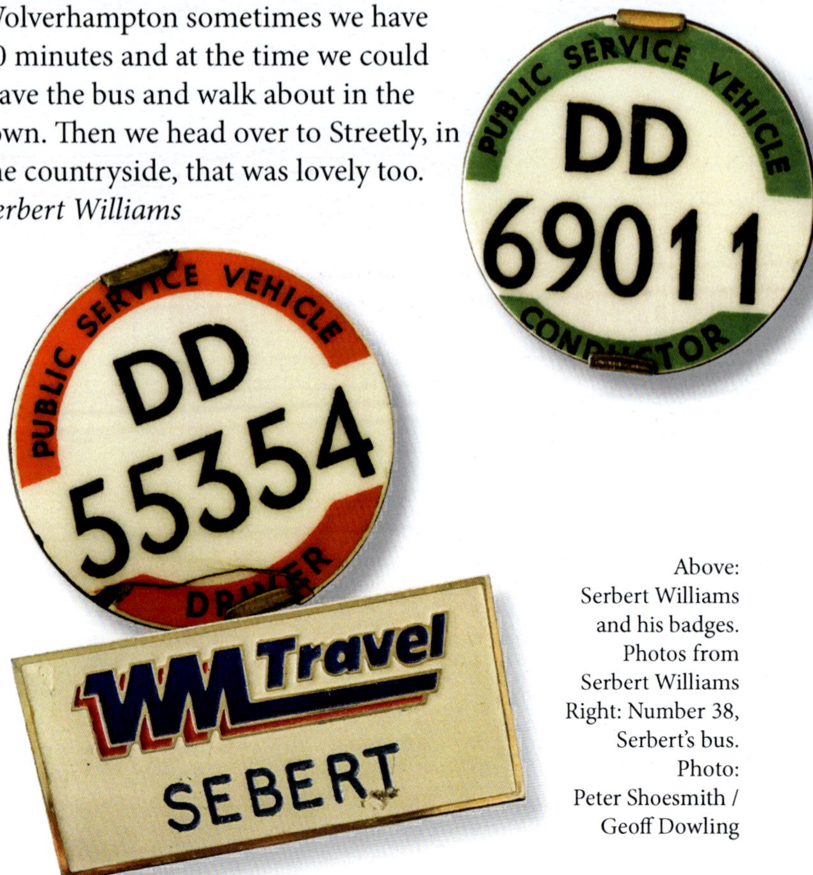

Above: Serbert Williams and his badges. Photos from Serbert Williams
Right: Number 38, Serbert's bus. Photo: Peter Shoesmith / Geoff Dowling

BROMWICH BUILDING SOCIETY
Please Pay On Entry
CHARLEMONT FARM ESTATE
38
BUSES LOAD HERE FOR 8 & 38
104
KEA 104E

She was blind, she said, 'Oh I don't like these blackies at all.' But I just couldn't hate her

I was working in the geriatrics hospital. I remember giving this lady a bath one day and she said, 'Oh if my husband knew that a black was giving me a bath he would go mad'. So I said to her, 'I'm sure he'll go mad today. A black is giving you a bath and you'll have one of the best baths in the world'.

I will tell you another instance. I went off to work this one afternoon and this nurse – she is a black girl but she was born here and she was soft spoken. She was giving out the tea and she said, 'Take this tea to this lady – Mrs Harris – she is blind'.

I took the tea to her and she said to me, 'Oh I don't like these blackies at all'. I said, 'Don't you Mrs Harris?' and she said, 'No'. I said, 'Do you know there is a blackie giving you this cup of tea'. She laughed.

In the afternoon I was giving her tea, her supper, because you had to feed her, and I said to her, I whispered in her ear, 'Guess who's here again? Your blackie'. And we laughed again.

So I gave her a cup of tea and we were laughing and her son came in. He said, 'Oh you're having a good laugh here now mother; what's it all about?' and I said, 'It's just a private joke between me and your mum'.

I loved that lady. After she left the hospital and went to a nursing home in Wednesbury, I went to visit her. I just couldn't hate her, I just said to her, 'Your black friend is here tonight'. I used to love her.

Joyce Nelson

Right: unknown nurse. Photo from Wikipedia
Below: Sandwell Hospital, 1960s. Photo from Hyacinth Jarrett

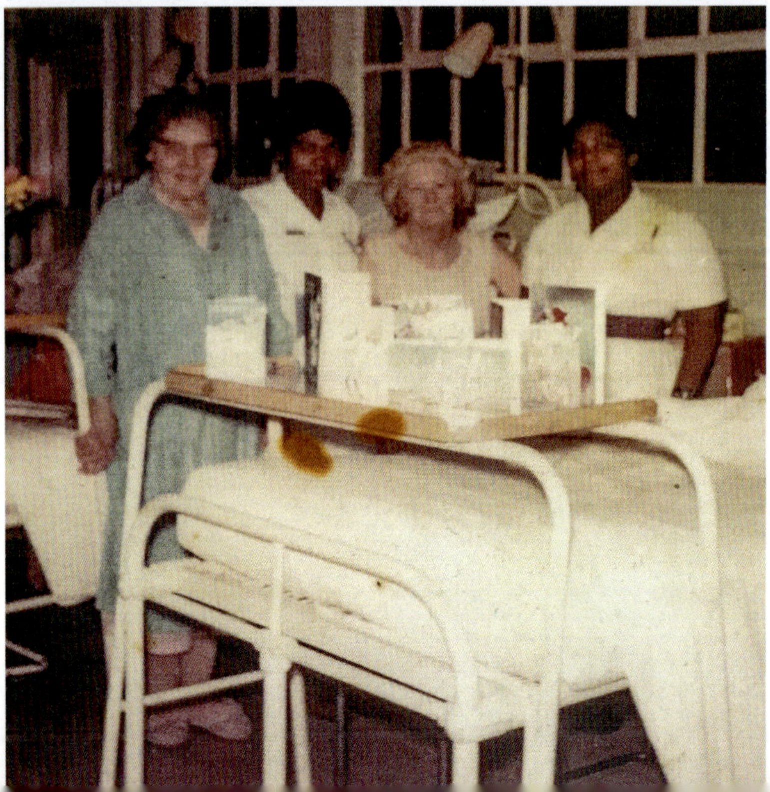

There was people on the side of the road, soldiers, almost every corner, with a rifle

18-year-old, bang, straight into Northern Ireland. That was my first experience in the armed forces. Now, Northern Ireland at that time was pretty serious. Early 70s, very serious. There was people on the side of the road, soldiers almost every corner, with rifles.

I didn't know much about Northern Ireland until I arrived, nobody tell you. Anyway, I met people, Irish people, who were saying, 'Oh, we have no fight with you, you know. Matter of fact, our history's the same'.

What I learned is how much our people, our ancestors, were involved in the armed forces, from the First to the Second World War, and now.

When you get told, 'Go back to your own country', and it did happen, I would have said, and I can confidently say it now, 'My ancestors fought for Britain. My ancestors gave aid to Britain, in terms of money, boats, aircraft, ambulances, oil, sugar, everything, to build Britain. So, I have a stake in Britain. So don't you tell me to go back anywhere, right'.

As a matter of fact, I was chosen to be an ethnic minority recruitment officer for the West Midlands and I did that for five years.

At schools, university, in the big square, I talked to youngsters about my life in the RAF as an engineer. I used to go round with an ejector seat, the stuff in it as well, showing how it worked. That was very satisfying, that was really good.
Don Campbell

Above: Belfast, 1969. Photo: Paul Hill
Right: Don Campbell Photo from Don Campbell

She shouldn't have said that because it's not true

In the end I gave up factory work. I ended up working in a care home. I'm getting abuse from the people I'm looking after and they'd be thumping you, spitting at you, calling you black and calling you all these terrible names they're not supposed to call you, and then you cannot do anything about it, you've just got to take it.

Then you come to a point where somebody says we come to take their jobs and I said, 'No, we didn't. We were sent for, to come and do jobs you didn't want to do. If you did want to do this job in the first place, they wouldn't have called us'. We nearly had a good bust up about it. I went really mad and somebody had to come and calm us down and they said, 'She shouldn't have said that because it's not true'.

Annette Simms

This page: The Colour Bar was a big issue even in the 1940s as shown by this English news magazine. It represented the glass ceiling for black people who had to tolerate low paid jobs along with abuse and little chance of promotion.
Opposite page: The Black Country, 1960s.
Photo: John Bulmer

HANSONS
SPECIAL
STOUT

Finding our feet

So we unite, all of us

Young white and black girls celebrating together in Bilston, 1957. Photo: David Bagnall Collection

Getting a mortgage was as difficult as going to the moon

My wages were £4.10 pence per week. But you look at it and you might laugh and say, '£4.10 pence, I wouldn't work for that'. But the men was getting £5. A loaf of bread was 2 pence, bus fare was 2 pence. Out of that money you could buy a house, because houses was £1,800 or £2,000. But it took a long time because the wages was very small, to save that much.

So we unite, all of us. That's how 'Partners' started. Partners was a group of people who needed money to buy a house or send kids to school. What we did was started putting whatever we could afford into a pool. Each person had a 'hand', like a share. It was like a Credit Union. It still goes on, it's just trust. We did it through trust, we didn't let each other down.

We used to help each other; it's still in us that if we see somebody that needs help you help that person, because you've been through it. And you never laugh at anybody who is down. Never look down. I never look down on anybody sitting on the ground begging or pass any sarcasm, because you don't know that person's life, what brought them to that. And I wouldn't pass without giving something. If I don't want to give them money, I'll buy them a meal or a drink. But I wouldn't pass somebody or look down on that person. And I've brought my kids up not to do it. And I'm bringing my grandkids up not to do it because it's probably no fault of his why he is there.
Hyacinth Jarrett

Yes, we had a mortgage. I mean both of us were working. So we had to try and put things together and try to get somewhere to live.
Joyce Nelson

Getting a mortgage was as difficult as going to the moon, you know. The first one that bought a house would actually rent the rooms out.
Errol Drummond

Jacqueline Jarrett,
Wattle Rd,
West Bromwich
Photo:
Hyacinth Jarrett

I felt like they said to us, ‘You can’t achieve anything much.’

In my last year at school, it was just like, ‘Oh, we have these kids, what are we going to do with them?’ and I quickly learned that there were no expectations in terms of taking an exam. So I didn’t get a choice. What they did was lumped you in with people who, some of them, barely spoke English. So it didn’t matter what your level of expectations were. It was like, ‘You ain’t gonna go there’. I felt like they said to us, ‘You can’t achieve anything much’.

But my calling was always the armed forces and it was from schooldays that I felt that. So I went and looked at the RAF. I walked in and it was a different welcome. I looked around and it started to sort of build. I told them what I wanted and they said, ‘Okay’. They asked a lot of questions about qualifications and this and that, as they do.

I got an appointment to go back and to do the attestation, which was Maths and English. They said, ‘At that appointment, if you get through it, then you do a medical. If you get through all of that, then you can join the armed forces’. So that’s what I did. When they said I would be working on aircraft, I asked, ‘Will I be travelling?’ I don’t think it actually plucked the heartstrings of my parents. ‘You’re going to join the Army? You’re going to get killed.’

In a very short space of time, I really did travel and, coming back, you know, when you’re sitting down, talking to them and all that, they just couldn’t believe what I’d done.
Don Campbell

School was a bit traumatic in the sense that having worked hard in Jamaica to go to a grammar school, I came to the UK and I was told that the grammar school was not of the same level, so I had to go to secondary modern. And my parents protested, you know, we fought it for a year or so, and in the end we actually won the battle for me to go to George Dixon, but by then I’d missed like two and a half, three years of it. So I thought what is the point in going just to be at the back of the class? That was my biggest disappointment and, perversely, most of us from the Caribbean believe that, at that level, the education standard in the Caribbean was actually higher.
Errol Drummond

Sunday School, Baptist Church, Fordhouses, (detail) Photo: Nick Hedges

Sunday School
Praise

When you're little and people are calling you names, it's hurtful

My grandad used to tell me things about when he first came to England from Jamaica.

He still struggled with things like racism to the point where he married my nan, who is a white woman, and she's English, British, and he had people writing on the walls of his house - things like 'go back home'.

When I was born, because I'm obviously mixed race, I'm quarter-caste - so my dad's white and my mom's half-caste - it was better then but, even when I was in primary school, I still had racism from people my own age. The children around you, they'd come out with stupid things like calling you 'chocolate brownie', when you're little and people are calling you names, it's hurtful.

My brother's also quarter-caste, and he's really pale, he's got like the African-Caribbean hair but really pale skin and, when he was little, he used to have people say to him, 'You're not mixed race, why are you saying that you're mixed race?' It used to upset my brother, and he used to say things like, 'Well, I'm brown on the inside'.

My grandad being fully Caribbean and my nan being fully white, they made mixed race children at the time when there wasn't really mixed race children, it just didn't happen.

They wanted to speak to my dad one of the nights after Guides, so my dad came in. I was stood next to him and the woman said, 'Where's your dad?' and I said, 'He's here'. She looked around my dad, who's a big person, and he said, 'I'm here' and she couldn't programme that my dad was white and my mom was mixed race and, even now, I get asked, 'Is your dad black?' and I say, 'No, he's white and my mom's black' and people can't understand. I don't understand why they ask me.

I think more than anyone, my family have said to me, 'It doesn't matter what a person's like, it's how they treat you and how you treat them'.

Lauren Campbell

Tantany Estate, West Bromwich, 1992
(from 'Tantany Talks', a youth project
with Racial Equality Council).
Courtesy of www.jubileeartsarchive.com

I used to think black people could never grow old!

I remember black people looking young. That's a very strange thing to say isn't it? But, if you think about it, our parents came here at a certain age. And as a young child I used to actually think that black people could never really age because across the road were all these white people that looked very aged! Now my children think I'm old!
Cllr Jackie Taylor

When people said, 'Where are all the old black people?' we said, 'We ate them! We nyam 'em!'
Mr Johns

We were the grandparent-less generation! They were left in the Caribbean so we had no grandparents to help look after the kids. We didn't have no things like washing machines either.
Hyacinth Jarrett

Right:
John and Joyce Nelson.
Photo from
Joyce Nelson.
Left:
The Black Country, 1960s
Photo: John Bulmer

What I'm proud of is my children

I had four lovely children from the marriage and I'm proud of them all because I pushed them to do things. I said, 'You can do that. I wasn't able to do it and you can, so you go and do that, go and get it done'.
Annette Simms

Mom and dad came here in the 1950s with nought but the shirt on their back, you know, the usual story. They didn't have anything to give us, so his philosophy, I suppose, was to make sure we could read and write and then we could learn the rest as we go along. He bought a set of Encyclopaedia Britannica. Looking back on it, I know we didn't have much money as a family, so that must have hurt.

Mom was an Avon Lady back in the 70s, and she used to get quite a lot of orders. We didn't have a calculator in those days and she used to come in with reams of paper with numbers on. I had to do all the adding up.
Lawrence Nelson

Me, I have ten alive. The Lord bless me with five girls and five boys. We want children because when you get older they can help. This week I had eleven grandchildren in my house, and my two daughters, oh yes.
Mavis Edwards-Stewart

As you get older you learn more. I had more experience than my mum had and she knows more than her mum does. It's generations and generations.

Now the children, what they know, it's out of this world! The knowledge they got I don't know where they get it from. Back home in Jamaica, we never start schooling until we were seven. But now you see kids going to school at two and a half. The world changes so much. How it comes about, I don't know, but somebody brings it about. I don't know who - if it's God or who, I don't know.
Stanley Simms

Above: Saturday school at Aklowa African school in Essex in Summer 1999. Aklowa aims to develop understanding of African Culture. The summer school was organised by the African-Caribbean Centre, West Bromwich. Many of this group went on to graduate.
Left: Joyce Nelson's son, Joseph, a professional musician.
Right: Stanley Simms' mantelpiece. Photo: Graham Peet

Still fighting racism

He said, ‘There will be rivers of blood!’

Enoch Powell, MP for Wolverhampton South West gave an infamous speech in 1968 talking about the rivers of blood that would result if immigration was not stopped.
Photo: Paul Hill

I've got loads of friends that are different races and I love 'em... I love all of them!

I actually worked on a midwifery ward, for experience. The way that people got treated, to me, it didn't seem fully right. There's a lot of things I think in the future need to change and I think they will eventually.

If you're a midwife, a lot of diverse people have babies and some people don't feel comfortable with certain races looking after them, which is discrimination.

But, if it's positive discrimination, for example Muslim women don't like non-Muslim people seeing them 'indecently'. I think they need more diverse workers to deal with a more diverse client.

I personally believe that you're not born racist. I think it's how you're brought up and what you're brought up around because I don't care what race you are, what religion you are, whether you're gay, straight, bisexual, whatever. I think it's down to your personality and nothing else really matters.

I've got loads of friends that are different races and I love 'em ... I love all of them!
Lauren Campbell

Sometimes, when dealing with racism, it's hard to determine whether you're being paranoid or if that's actually a 'thing'. Because so many people are 'pulling the race card', a lot of people take it lightly. And sometimes you need a second opinion to be like, 'Am I imagining this, or is this really happening?' And I think if you've got other black people, or union reps or whatever, then they might have experienced something similar or they might be like, 'Nah, you're over-reacting'. So you don't want to pull the race card for no reason.

I would never say that someone was racist unless I had that concrete evidence because it's not a nice thing to say to anyone, d'ya know what I mean? Especially if they didn't mean it like that.

With black people, especially Jamaicans, they don't really encourage homosexual behaviour. They don't really stand for it at all. I think it's one of them things where times have changed. That's just life man. Get over it.
Rose Wilkins

Mrs Whynne and her best friend, bottling plant, Unigate Dairy, 1977. Photo: Nick Hedges

Unigate

They would shout, 'Speak English! It's a cuppa tae!'

My biggest problem really was communication. The workers, they were Black Country men but when I went to the work's canteen to buy my breakfast, there was about a hundred people or more and when I used to say, 'OK, toast, bacon sandwich and a cup of tea, please', they would shout out, 'Speak English! It's a cuppa tae!' and then I would say, 'A drink of water'. They'd say, 'Speak English! It's waerter!' It took a very long time to get into the Black Country accent.
Kenneth James

Living in Sandwell as a black man, I've seen everything. I've seen absolutely everything. If you go to the market you'll be speaking to a Chinese guy, a black guy. They all have the same accent!
Anthony McFarlane

My teacher, and the whole class, was absolutely and completely obsessed with my accent, he even gave me a microphone and told me to speak. And I didn't even know what to say so I said to him, 'Wha me fi say?'. You know, because they just wanted me to speak; they were obsessed.

All of a sudden, I'm mixed in with all these different nationalities: Asians, as in Pakistanis, Indians and then the range of the different Caribbean islands, which I wasn't exposed to before.
Don Campbell

I'm not Jamaican. I've never been to Jamaica but I can speak patois. Patois is like an accent. It's like Black Country. If I'm at work I speak proper Black Country cuz I'm with Bilston people. I'm with Tipton people. You just do it subconsciously.

With my generation, if you're born in the 90s, our slang is almost derived from patois, so it's like even my white friends will talk it. It's all mixed up. But then again patois is like that anyway, it comes from Spanish, English, Creole.
Rose Wilkins

Tea at engineering company,
Willenhall, Walsall, 2011.
Photo: Martin Parr / Magnum Photos

White people can be friendly, but be a snake - you get me?

I heard there was a lot of racism back in the day, a lot of racism. I heard stories that black people and Irish people and 'darks' should not go into a shop, I heard that kind of story. Basically, when I came here and my mom told me that, it made me have a different image, view of white people.

I can remember the first time I came here, went to the park, just to play football. Me, I came from Jamaica - that's what I like - went to the park, playing some football, seen these two white ladies. I was looking at them, waved at them and that, I'm thinking it's a friendly environment. About twenty minutes after that, there was police all over the park; them come up to me, asking all kinds of information like, 'Who are you, where you from?' So I don't know why it was that relevant, for me to be in the park, playing ball and police coming all up there, surrounding me, asking who I am, what's my name, what's my date of birth. Since then, since that happened, I've had a different view of white people, cuz when I came, I used to say, 'Oh, white people are friendly' but since that happened to me I say, 'White people can be friendly but be a snake - you get me - they can be friendly, they can smile in your face, and then they be a snake behind your back, you don't know what they're thinking'.

Well, me, I'd rather have signs saying I shouldn't go there, innit? More than someone trying to prison me, trying to make me go to prison. You know when you go somewhere, trying to do something positive and they just phone the police and try to make it negative, everything's become negative.

Racism is still about but it's more of a thing. It's not like back in the days like when they used to tell you not to go to places. In our days it's more of a thing where it's just in their heart; they're not telling you, but it's in their heart.

Oniel Wright

I have members of my family who are very smart and should be highly successful, law abiding citizens. Instead they are in prison serving long sentences. Black people are massively over-represented in prison and we have to ask, 'Why?'

Kurly McGeachie

Outside the Unemployment Centre, High Street, West Bromwich, 1986 (from 'The Golden Mile' Exhibition). Photo: Peter Singh, Michael Richards, John Gayle Courtesy of www.jubileeartsarchive.com

GB
945 MOH

This is not what you think

We were here when the National Front came up to Cronehills school and I remember we all sat there, me and my mates, black, white, Asian, going, 'Oh, I didn't know you did that. OK. OK'.

The St George's Day Parade - my mate runs that, Mark; he's great. I remember saying, 'Oh, we're going to do something with St George's Day'. And I got an email from the council asking if I was aware of this group? 'Oh, yes, I'm aware', I said, 'You've got it wrong. This is not what you think. They're celebrating St George's Day as a group of people and if you look at the photographs, there's Indian people there, there's black people there'. I said, 'It's about a group of people celebrating their history and their pride'. I love Sandwell because it's not segregated.
Anthony McFarlane

I'm not so sure about this. They used to say, 'There ain't no black in the Union Jack'. Doesn't that say something about what they were thinking? I think its just much more complicated!
Shane Ward

It was quite an experience coming to this country, the different culture but, luckily, where I was working we called it the United Nation because there was people from every country ... Russian, Polish, Hungarian, all the Caribbean Islands - Jamaica, Trinidad, Barbados - that was the United Nation. There was lots of Italians and there was only two English man doing the the same job as us. Everyone else was in charge. Every English man was electrician, plumber, welder, engineer but only two man was working with us on the furnace, two English man.
Kenneth James

Above: St George's Day, West Bromwich, 2010.
Photo: Martin Parr / Magnum

Above: West Bromwich Market,
Brett Packer selling clothes, 2010.
Photo: Martin Parr / Magnum

Keeping body and soul together

When we used to go to the English church, we were not welcome

Testimony at an
Episcopal church service,
Wolverhampton, 1976.
Photo: Nick Hedges

That's why black people started off buying their own church

Years and years ago it did happen; you weren't welcome. That's why black people started off buying their own church, built their own church and make sure they have their own church because when we used to go to the English church, we weren't made welcome.

Some did, but some of them you were not, so that's why they ended up starting in their houses and then from there, they get their own church.
Annette Simms

Some churches, they wouldn't allow blacks in, so you start a church in the houses. You get married, you have to have a reception in the front room of where you live. I did my wedding myself, set the table, do sandwiches, everything. And you have to do that yourself, and you have to clean it up and set it back before you even go to bed. I dressed my husband and send him off to church. Send him off to the church. We got married at the Evangelical Church in Langley.
Hyacinth Jarrett

Pastor Joseph greets his congregation,
Wolverhampton, 1976.
Photo: Nick Hedges

Young woman singing in a Baptist church service,
Fordhouses, Wolverhampton, 1976.
Photo: Nick Hedges

The pain I was in, was gone

When I was recovering from my hip replacement, one morning I was praying and fasting. This lady where we were praying was walking around. She was looking at my feet and then she was at my feet and praying and rubbing. A couple of hours after I came home, do you know, the pain I was in was gone. I could walk without pain.
Annette Simms

I go to church a lot! Oh my goodness yes. All I need is a duvet!
Marva Nisbett

I did make sure my children went to Sunday School but then they came to the age where they didn't want to go anymore, I couldn't force them to go. But they know what is right and what is wrong, so they do know God.

My youngest some time back said, 'My friend's daughter is ill, can you pray for her?'

I talk to them but I don't push it on them, I don't push it down their throat.
Annette Simms

Ladies' Day, the Bethel Convention Centre, West Bromwich, 2010. Photo: Martin Parr / Magnum Photos

Helping us to help ourselves

For me as a councillor, one of the most important jobs is to support all the amazing things that the community do for themselves. Hugely important in this are the organisations that have grown up in Sandwell and the Black Country to help people to help themselves. I want to pay tribute to some of these organisations so that in times to come people can see what a vibrant and important role they played in making our community.

Here are some, but perhaps not all:
West Bromwich African-Caribbean Resource Centre; OSCAR; ACCO; Tolunka; Sandwell African-Caribbean Mental Health Foundation - Kuumba; Sandwell African-Caribbean Forum; Sandwell African-Caribbean Consultative Body; Sandwell Tipton African-Caribbean Forum; African-Caribbean Improvement Service; Community Action Project; Sandwell and District West Indian Community Association.
Cllr Jackie Taylor

Wolverhampton Show, Inspirational Ladies Group, 2012.
Gloria Hamilton (left) and Lucida Dull (right).
Photo: Martin Parr / Magnum Photos

The
Inspirational
Ladies Group
The
Inspirational
Ladies Group

I haven't got no money but I feel rich when I come here

In the 80s, that's when the West Bromwich African-Caribbean Resource Centre was open. I used to go there at events and they asked me to become a trustee.

I also become a member of the Labour Party, which is a paid-up member. I met with MPs and councillors and would have meetings and I was sitting on the selection committee to select people to become councillors.

I remember that big champion that we had to kick out racism - Billy Bragg - he came to the Caribbean Centre and about a hundred of us went around the area and deliver leaflets and T-shirts saying, 'kick racism out!'
Kenneth James

I struggle a bit, I tell you no lies. I did struggle a bit with my children when they was small. A real hard struggle. Struggle, struggle. But I manage. My aunty, died and gone, she was like a mother to me.

I will never forget the support when my son died. The support from this Caribbean Centre and the people in West Bromwich. This is my second home, and I'm glad for it.

I haven't got no money but I feel rich when I come here - the greeting, the welcome that I get, it's good enough for me.
Miss U

We wanted somewhere where we could come. You could have the weddings. You can have church. You can have parties and things like that. Most of us who didn't want to go to pubs, or the noise was too much, we come here because it was quiet. And you were looked after, you feel safe. Some of the older members don't even want new ones to come in. They moan. You have to make an argument with them to say, 'Listen, people have to come in. It's for the public'. We have the home care service and we care for children as well. We have the day centres for the elderly which is good. We used to run a youth club, but we lost the funding.

Now we are trying our best to get funding. It's hard. Very hard. I'm hoping that it won't come to a stage where it will close. I hope not, because it would be such a big blow. So many people would miss it.
Hyacinth Jarrett

Maisy enjoying a meal at the African-Caribbean Resource Centre. She is on page 95 too, as a sixteen year old, with Muhammad Ali! 2016
Photo: Graham Peet

NY

A comfortable place where they can feel safe

I've been producing, singing, rapping and doing music workshops for over 10 years. During that time, I did a course which is for women that have gone through domestic violence.

They get to go to my studio and literally just express whatever, it doesn't have to be specific domestic violence issues. You can do whatever you need to but it's just a place where they can come to where there's no men involved, it's run by women for women. They can just be relaxed. They don't have to do their hair, don't have to worry about their nails. They don't have to think about whatever. The most thing they're going to have to think about is what time to go and pick up the kids. They've got a comfortable place where they can feel safe and they can get some stuff off their chest.

Justice Holtec

The Hidden Girl, 2013.
Photo: Herbert Walters

People look at it as you're possessed, you've got demons

It's been challenging sometimes. Going to church doesn't exempt you from struggles of life, family issues but it gave us a point of reference to say, 'Look, we have to try and maintain a good sense of well-being because we're a Christian family'.

There is definitely an issue within churches, particularly the denominational faith background that I'm from. I think people look and think you're possessed, you've got demons and all that stuff. Even if you were to turn that context on its head, mental health isn't just what would be considered 'acting crazy' or losing your mind. Sometimes mental health can be as simple as you're not feeling up to your normal self and there are people in the Bible, to use a theological approach, who had struggles. There were people like King David, Job. Even Jesus said, 'My soul is exceeding sorrow from its death'. Now that is, for me, the crescendo.

If even Jesus has gone through mental and physical pain and struggle, but has overcome, then it doesn't mean that mental health has to be this scary thing. It's something that all of us, everybody, in some way, shape, or form has got to deal with, we've got to manage our own well-being and make sure that we're okay.

I think it was something to do with some of the stress I was under. Towards the end of secondary school, I developed mental health issues and problems and stuff. It's classed now as bipolar disorder. The first episode, if you like, was when I was 16 years old. As far as I can remember, I think with the GCSEs and that sort of stuff, it always became a trigger and I just totally lost it. Started acting oddly.

I remember at 16, it scared the whole family, jumping out of a window in the middle of the night. Out of my bedroom window. I was awake. I thought I could fly.
Jeremy Grant

Young boy testifying at the African
Methodist Church of Zion,
Wolverhampton, 1976.
Photo: Nick Hedges

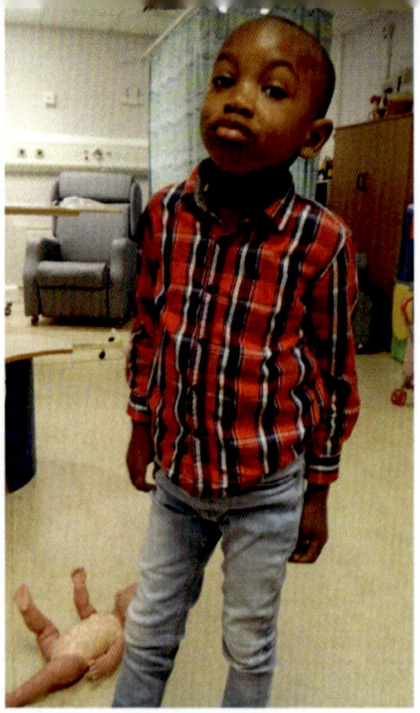

Why will the child that's so innocent have to go through so much?

I went to City Hospital and the nurse, she sat down and she said, 'We've tested you and you've got the thalassemia trait' and I said, 'I don't even know what that is'.

So, going through the normal route the baby came. And one day I got a letter from the children's hospital that I should take the baby for a heel prick.

The nurse came to my house and I said to her, 'You can sit down' but she said, 'No, you sit down'. So I was wondering what kind of news she'd come with as she was telling me to sit down. She said to me, 'We've tested the baby and he's fully sickle cell'.

She went through with me what's liable to happen with the child and stuff and I was just wondering, 'Why will the child that's so innocent have to go through so much?'

I got a letter to go to children's hospital. They were very good; they told me what to expect and everything. He didn't have any problem when he was small. Every year he's got to do a brain scan to see, because these sufferers, they can develop a stroke in the brain that we are not aware of.

The only time you'd be aware is when you see the child start to change, like, in behaviour or getting slower than what you expect of them. It doesn't bother him at this age, it's when he gets into the teenage stage.

So, being a single parent, it's sometimes scary, like, when he's ill and the first thing I want to do is panic and then I say, 'No, I can't panic. I have to do what I have to do'.

So, you see, being taught what to expect, and I do my research, and then I'm here at OSCAR; I've had full support from them. Sometimes I'm not even in work now because if I'm working, and he gets ill, I have to come home, you know?

At school, sometimes they call me out, 'Oh, Tray is having pains', and then I have to go and get him. Sometimes it's kind of stressful because I would really love to work full-time and stuff but I can't. If he's ill, I can't work, I can't get money then things start backfiring and stuff.

That is why I come here and volunteer. If I didn't have this place to turn to, I don't know how I would manage.

Alison Brown

Above:
Photo of Tray
by Alison Brown

Children and families helped by
Sandwell Sickle Cell and Thalassaemia Centre, (SCAT)
Organisation for Sickle Cell Anaemia Research, (OSCAR)
Photo: OSCAR

I think there's been a bit of a politician in me, all my life

Even as a child, I used to say, 'This can't be right.' Watching Harold Wilson talking on the black and white TV screen with his pipe, I used to try and take an interest, but then play would take over.

Much later on, I remember having discussions with women of my road. They'd comment about the road, it could be about the uneven pavement, the litter, then the conversation would move on to certain other things like transport for example, and I found myself making contact with Sandwell Council on behalf of these individuals, and would soon realise that all it took was a phone call and you could get that difficulty sorted.

Then I just got involved with going to local branch meetings in the ward, and then just gradually got involved with putting myself forward.

It was 2014 when I was elected as a councillor. To be the first black, African-Caribbean female councillor is a real privilege. But the journey isn't just for me. I'm hoping that I can carry other people of colour along with me as well. I hope that other people will join me in this journey. My fellow councillors, my peers on the council have been absolutely phenomenal, they really have. I tell you we are a family.
Cllr Jackie Taylor

I am and always have been proud of Jackie. She has always been kind, caring and sharing and always fighting for what is right.
Richard Bair, Jackie Taylor's father

Left:
Cllr Jackie Taylor, on her way to becoming a politician.
Right:
Handsworth conversation, 1972.
Photo: George Hallett, Library of Birmingham

African Museum
STUDIO ONE
Produced by C.S. Dodd
RECORDED AT JAMAICA RECORDING STUDIO, KINGSTON, JAMAICA
85 West Street,
Kingston, Jamaica.
VERSION
SOLOMONIC
Pub. Solomonic B.M.I.
DISTR. BY SOLOMONIC DISTRIBUTOR
VERSION
BUNNY WAILER
UNAUTHORISED COPYING IS PROHIBITED
POWER HOUSE
Mftd. & Dist. by Sonic Sounds 14 Retirement Road, Kgn. 5. Ph. 62036-61204
Made in Jamaica
Pro. by Sly & Robbie Taxi Production
LEFT BACK
ALL RIGHTS RESERVED — MADE IN JAMAICA
45 RPM
MADE IN JAMAICA
Dist by: Black Roots Record 1 Robert Cres., Kgn. 5.
Produced, arranged and directed by Kwame Heshimu
CHANTI
Made in Jamaica
STEREO
CMI-002B
Pub.: Chanti Music Inc.
© ℗ 1979
Eng.: Phillip Smart
BEAST OF BURDEN
(Kwame Heshimu)
TINMAN RHYTHM SECTION
All Rights Reserved. Unauthorised Duplication is a Violation of applicable Laws
CRAZY JOE
Phone: 92-22386
Records 24 Retirement Cres., Kingston 5. and distributed at 20 North Parade
ALL NIGHT LONG
(Errol T. — H. Williams)
HERMAN WILLIAMS
UNAUTHORISED COPY OF THIS RECORDING IS STRICTLY PROHIBITED
Black & White
SIDE B
Prod. By C. Patterson
45 R.P.M.
GAMES MAN SKANK
Carlton Patterson
KING TUBBYS
UNAUTHORISED COPYING OF THIS RECORDING IS
Technique
LIGHTNING
Produced & Arranged by: Stepping King Miguel
(P) 1980
(C) 1980
DREAD
at the controls

In Jamaica there is music, there is parties, there is street music everywhere

We had nowhere to go because there was no clubs, so what we used to do is visit each other on a Sunday afternoon. We visit each other, we prepare a meal, and you have a friend or a relative come and spend the afternoon. And we play music. And the music was pretty loud.

We are a people who has music, and always have music. In Jamaica there is music, there is parties, there is street music everywhere, so you are used to it. And it uplifts people because that's part of our culture. Singing calypso and dancing and eating food and drinking. The men drink, you know. Most of the women didn't drink.
Hyacinth Jarrett

Yes, well those days you couldn't afford a radio. You started to get these – I think they called them Blue Spot – but you would have a little radio.
Joyce Nelson

Where we grew up there were only about five black families on the whole estate. When we moved to this side of town, I said, 'There's a lot of black people round here, mum. There's loads of them. Wow'. So for me there was an experience of learning about what our culture was. They were into reggae music. I was into Motown and Rock 'n' Roll. So I grew up going to Rock 'n' Roll clubs, dancing Rock 'n' Roll with my mates and then we all discovered Motown and then from Motown we all got into Northern Soul.
Anthony McFarlane

Above: A Blue Spot Radiogram. Photographer unknown.

Music for a church service,
Wolverhampton, 1976.
Photo: Nick Hedges

We used to discuss the world and what was going on

There used to be a place in West Bromwich where I used to go for a blues, and it was a house, and we used to go there every Friday night. It's still there. There used to be the Sportsman, a club in West Brom, that used to be my Friday night haunt. It's the reference points. We used to hang in West Brom town centre in the top precinct. There was loads of black guys. That was our place to meet. We used to roller skate through there. We used to discuss the world and what was going on.
Anthony McFarlane

Now we've got this instant age where you can just rap on your phone and put it up and everyone's like, 'Oh my God, it's so amazing', we've gotten to the point were we've stopped researching. Researching doesn't mean that you find something and it's okay. It means that you should be able to take the knowledge that we've built as a people. Now there's young people that I speak to that maybe don't have that point of reference. The information is not out there. Back in the day, say they couldn't go to certain songs that would just be in your culture. So you'd pass that on to your little sister, for your older cousin, for your auntie etc, but with social media because it makes you isolated, you're just on your phone. Your cousin is on their phone, your aunties, your mum's even got an app!
Justice Holtec

Above: Aeon Anderson, aged 10, at the Black Patch adventure playground, Smethwick. He was later to become rapper MC/Doctor Funk and play a major part in developing the West Midland's Hip Hop scene. Photo: Martin Jones
Right: Crazy Spades breakdance group, Windmill Lane Community Centre, Smethwick, 1984. Courtesy of www.jubileeartsarchive.com

Years go by, you just get caught up in the streets, you get me?

Learning about street music is good. Living in the street, doing music; a lot of things go on in the street.

I seen some guys around on the corner chilling and I think it was cool because they rap and they look like gangsters, so I said to myself, 'OK, let me go chill with them'. Years go by, you just get caught up in the streets, you get me? That feeling you get like you need to go there, it's like an addiction, it's like something bringing you back there. It's not a good thing.

When I was growing up, we never used to chill with white people. I'm not gonna lie, we used to chill with just a group of black guys just standing on the corner. People walk past, they look at us, they scared. That used to make me feel good, I used to feel good about it, to know that people scared of me, you get me? But after a while, you look at people - I mean you see a nice looking girl and you probably go up to her and she just, she's running away from you 'cos everybody's just scared of you, you get me? Sometimes I seen nice people I want to talk to but because of my image, they look at me like, oh I'm just a gangster, so they don't want nothing to do with you.

I got a friend that got stabbed, that died, so basically I don't see no future in that, I don't see no future in the streets.
Oniel Wright

You could get sidetracked into things, like robbing. I had a lot of other friends who ended up in jail.

Sounds was something to do, if we were involved in a bit of robbery, you have to remember, in those days we used to like steal sheets of wood to make a box.

You start off with one box and a little amp. We used to meet down at the garage and like mess about, it built from there. Our first dance ever was in Chain Walk, in Lozells. It was like roots, rock reggae, dub, that sort of thing. Sounds sort of brought us together, it gave us a focus then.
John Siffa

When I was young, I wanted to be a gangster, chillin', but right now it's about making money.
Akinwande Phillips

Siffa Sound System, Handsworth Park. From the left: Ricoh, President, Bandit, Libby and General, 1983. Photo: Vanley Burke

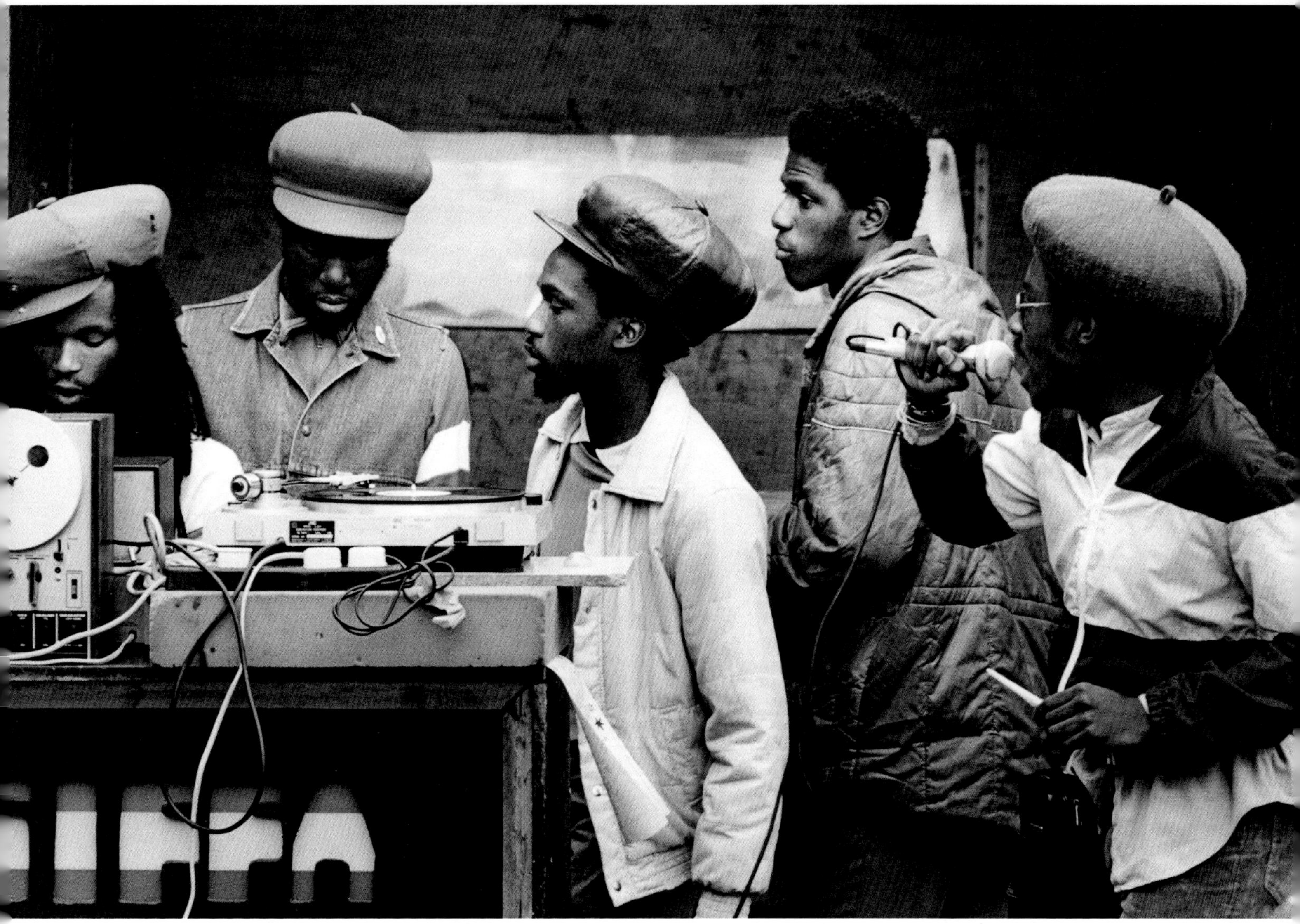

Us black guys, we don't feel good in our own skin no more

Me, I can go Wednesbury now, where there's a lot of white people in the area. If I go over there right now, you'd never find me go in the pub and sit down and have a drink, nev-er, that's not gonna happen. I tried it one time, with my black girlfriend, went in there ... everybody's staring at me like just sharking me. I just left. So basically, most of us black guys, we don't feel good in our own skin no more.

I know a lot of guys are bleaching. Even in Jamaica, that made the black females have to be bleaching, because if a black female ain't bleaching, there's nobody looking at them - you get what I'm trying to say? And if they don't go to the hair salon and buy that extension fake weave, there's no-one looking at them. So black females go through harder than us, if they go out on the street, and they ain't got their extension in, they don't feel comfortable.
Oniel Wright

And white people, they can't wait to get a tan, or get fake tan!
Don Campbell

Black hair was never recognised, never recognised. The amount of damage that used to be done with the perms and things, because by rights the perms was not supposed to be sold. It was because of the strength of it. And it damaged. Your head is sore, your skin is sore, it oozes water. It's horrible to see what it does to the skin.

It's the same with the bleach. It's illegal to sell the bleach because it's causing cancer and a lot more. If your skin breaks and you put it on, it will be surprising to what it will do with your body. But because it's blacks who uses it mainly, the government don't bother. It's hidden at the back of the shop but the government don't actually enforce the law.
Hyacinth Jarrett

Sandwell Show, West Bromwich, 2010. Photo: Martin Parr / Magnum Photos

Alex Stlyes
Hairdresser. West
Bromwich, 2010.
Photo: Martin Parr /
Magnum Photos

Some of our black heroes

Goldie and graffiti crew at Heath Town, Wolverhampton, 1980s.
Photo: Dave Bagnall

AUTO

The barmaid pointed to me and said, 'You know we don't serve coloured people here'

Malcolm X was fighting racism in the US and he was an international figure who did a lot of work in the States. The Indian Workers' Association resolved to invite him to Smethwick. We invited him to come and support the struggle of the people fighting against racism in Britain and particularly in Smethwick where there was an overt colour bar against Asians and African-Caribbeans in public houses, barber shops, hotels, restaurants, estate agents. So with this background I met him on Marshall Street on the corner of St Paul's Road. There were also journalists and TV cameras. We met and briefly we talked about what he intended to do here. His wish was that he simply wanted to walk up and down Marshall Street on his own and see what happens.

On the way up he saw a poster in an estate agent window, 'House for sale. No coloured people need apply'. He talked with an African-Caribbean man for a while. When he walked back there was a crowd of white women; they shouted a few abusive languages but he didn't take any notice. Then he said he wanted to see a pub where the colour bar was being practised. So, I, along with my two colleagues, took him to a pub. We went into the smoke room where the colour bar was operated and I ordered four drinks and the barmaid pointed to me and said, 'You know we don't serve coloured people here'. No argument, we walked out and through Stony Lane to the Blue Gates pub and went into the bar and there he had a drink. He met more people of colour sitting there. Then he made a statement about how shocked he was. It was in the papers and on the TV.
Avtar Singh Jouhl

I like Malcolm X. I'm thinking about getting a quote of his tattooed. Probably on my ribs.
Rose Wilkins

I always get this feeling if I was sat round there now and there was Marcus Garvey and there was Malcolm X they'd be looking at us and they'd be going, 'What you doing? Why do you think we did all this? We did all this so you could take the ball and you could move us on'.
Anthony McFarlane

Above:
Malcolm X visiting
Smethwick, 1965.
Photographer unknown.

Right:
Malcolm X poster in
Handsworth.
Designer unknown.

I'm inspired!

I'm inspired by Bob Marley, Will Smith even Stormzy as well; Vybz Kartel, even though they say he's a bad person, but I'm still inspired by him in some ways, in the good ways he's good at music.
Oniel Wright

Top: Ivor Linton, from West Brom, played for Aston Villa. Photo: Keith Hayley, Popperfoto
Opposite: Muhammad Ali and Maisy at the Muhammad Ali Centre, Birmingham, August,1983. Photo from Maisy Benain
Left: Bob Marley T-shirts, West Brom market.
Below: The Three Degrees pop group with West Bromwich Albion footballers' Laurie Cunningham, Brendan Batson and Cyrille Regis. Photo: Brian Bould/ANL/REX/Shutterstock
Denise Lewis from West Brom, winning gold medal Heptathlon 2000 Olympics. Photo: Getty Images

Now we're a part of the community

I'm good enough to open my own business

Home from Home, High St., West Bromwich, 2016. Photo: Graham Peet

£1·20p
£1·99p
Nurishment
Original
Vanilla
Big Bamboo
Jamaican
Irish Moss
284 ml
£1·20
Grace
Coconut Water
Genuine Caribbean Taste
LSV
LSV energy drink
Supermalt
Original
75p
89p
Sun exotic
KA
Pineapple
Strawberry
Fruit Punch
Barr
Cream Soda
Tango
Mighty Malt
Original
99p
leap in the dark

Where's the black food?

In Sandwell there was no race relations board or anything. There was no black food. We started, three of us... Mrs Ford - Edith Ford, she used to work for the council - and Mrs Sandhu, Asian lady - she had a shop in New Street - and my shop was in Bull Street. There was no black food. The only thing we could get was bananas. And when we said we needed black food, to try and get the government to allow it to be imported, they said we had to prove it. So we go out at night, because everybody's working, so you have to go when they come from work, for a survey. There was one shop that used to sell the banana, Ted ... that was his greengrocery on the high street. There was no race relation board. There was no trading standards. So I was part of getting those in.

They started bringing in yam, sweet potatoes and things like that. Black people want black food. Before, it was just potatoes, but they hated spud. It was just rice, flour, spud. You couldn't get anything. It wasn't coming into Britain at all. I helped to bring it in.
Hyacinth Jarrett

Green bananas and yams. There would be not a lot of breadfruit – as it is now. You used to get breadfruit in the tin and yam in a tin. It wasn't very nice. But of course it reminded you of home. And then, later on, you started getting sweet potatoes and different things. When we came here first we couldn't get those but as time went on we started getting them.
Joyce Nelson

I had this impression of tasting baked beans for the first time and thinking, 'What is this? How can anyone eat this?'

It was so different because I had all the different peas and beans and whatever in the Caribbean and none of them were like that. Your gungo peas, your red peas, your black-eyed peas, whatever. They were all quite savoury. They weren't sweet like baked beans.

When somebody gave me baked beans, I was like, 'What is this?' but I didn't quite say it like that; having just come from Jamaica, it was, 'Wha' dis?'
Don Campbell

Above: Jackson's Caribbean Groceries, Kings Square, West Bromwich, 2016. Photo: Graham Peet

Luncheon club at the African-Caribbean Centre, West Bromwich, 1988, (from 'Bickle' exhibition). Photo: Maxine Walker / Nigel Madhoo Courtesy of www.jubileeartsarchive.com

You can always tell what the area is depending on their takeaways... it's true, it is!

West Brom is very, very diverse. For example, Dudley - I know it sounds crazy but - there's a lot of chip shops, the Black Country have a lot of chip shops! But West Brom have a lot of Caribbean takeaways and a lot of Indian takeaways, and then the odd chip shop, so you can always tell what the area is, depending on their takeaways. It's true, it is! The people around here supply for the people that live here!
Lauren Campbell

Chloe Thomas, Top Taste Caribbean Takeaway, West Bromwich, 2016. Photo: Graham Peet

ITAL IRISH MASH
OKRA JUICE
CANNED DRINKS
JUNE PLUM JUICE
MORNING PRAYER
JAMAICAN TASTE
CARIBBEAN TAKEAWAY
Stew Chicken • Curry Goat • Jerk Chicken
Oxtail • Ackee & Saltfish • Fried Chicken
Fried Fish • Soup • and much more...
Jamaican Snacks
also on sale
No

Baking Caribbean bread in Smethwick

Post Windrush, there was an influx. In those days, when I came here, when I walked through Handsworth, I was surprised at the amount of Caribbean people that lived there. Not so much today but, in those days, a lot. So of course there was a market. I think Sunrise Bakery was one of about half a dozen bakeries that serviced this part of the West Midlands.

What they did, they targeted their core market which was Caribbean people anyway, so what they made was the bread and buns and cakes that we had in the Caribbean, so it was a bit of a home from home if you like. Everything was made by hand, it was very much a craft bakery.

Only the process changes, you know, bread is basically flour, water and yeast. It's just the process that makes it different and the bread they made is called a hard dough bread which is not as firm as a baker let's say. Probably like an Irish soda dough type of texture.

I felt personally that with the rise of the supermarket you would actually see the demise of our more traditional retailers, like the corner shops. They were our only route to market, if you like. Asda started in 1966, the same year as the bakery. They've had a lot more success mind! But, you know, we got into Asda and, in turn, Tesco, Sainsbury's, Morrisons.

Errol Drummond

Errol Drummond, left, and David Fisher, right. The Sunrise Bakery, Smethwick, 2016. Photos: Graham Peet

SUNRISE BAKERY
Caribbean Style
HARD DOUGH
BREAD 800g

I was the top, 100%. I'd passed 100%!

I decided I'm not going to work for anybody, I'm going to work for myself. And I thought - go to college. I rang up and applied and made an appointment for an interview to see if I could get into the college in Wolverhampton to do hairdressing. They didn't think I was black and when I went and they saw that I was, they did everything to dis-encourage me not to come, because they didn't think that I would be able to do it, because they'd never had a black student before. And I said to them, 'I'll take the test. If I fail the test I'll never bother you but, if I pass the test, I'm going to be here'. I passed the test and I went. It should have been a three year course, and I was that good I did it in a year and a half.

I remember when I did the perming and I went in on the following morning and, when I looked, the board was up. Before I could get in the classroom, the secretary was on top of the stairs and said, 'It had to be you. Nobody else but you'. And I thought I hadn't done anything so why did she have to say that. And when I went in and look at the board I was the top. 100%. I'd passed 100%. And everybody was coming, 'We've heard of ninety-six, ninety-seven, never a bloody hundred before'.

I was offered a teaching position at the college. I thought if I'm offered a teaching position, I'm good enough to open my own business.

I went to the principal and said, 'What do you think? I want to open a business, do you think I will be a success?', and he said, 'Hyacinth, if you are not successful it's you who do not want to do it, but you're bloody good. So go for it'. And I did. And I never looked back. Forty years. I was the first black person to open a business in Sandwell.

Hyacinth Jarrett

Above: Hyacinth Jarrett
Right: her hairdressing salon, West Bromwich.
Photos: Hyacinth Jarrett and Shane Ward

Black
beauty &
hair
Summer 1984 £1.25
SIZZLING
Sunny styles
Summer fashion

Not again!

I am really fearful that it is happening again

Vicarage Road, Smethwick, 1962. Photo: Birmingham Black Oral History Project

Go back to Britain of the 1950s, every face is exactly the same colour. You know, that is not Britain now

We're living and working in very interesting times, where, for a second term, this government has been voted in and I am just bereft by all of that, because I really don't believe that people recognise what has been done and what is about to happen.

We as a Labour Party have got a lot of work to do and I think if we can unite we can get this government out, we have to get this government out. Come to my surgery. I've had a woman ... I can't believe in this day and age ... absolutely starving, yeah, because she's been homeless with her baby in her arms. I couldn't believe that her benefits had been stopped. Then the man with throat cancer, a man who has a family, had his benefits stopped, not cut! Not slashed in half, just stopped, because he's got throat cancer but he can walk.

You know, there are people in the workplace being bullied. You can see that's the fire within my belly. I'm not having it. Justice, equality, fairness, compassion.
Cllr Jackie Taylor

As Jamaicans, I think we are inextricably linked with Birmingham and the Black Country. Even going back to the days of slavery, right, because on the bad side of it a lot of the implements of slavery were actually manufactured in Birmingham. And we had a lot of the abolitionists, abolitionist people like those involved with the Lunar Society. Your Cadburys, your Wedgwoods and people like that. They led the forefront of abolitionists.

It was sad in a sense that they've been sold a perception that you leave Europe and you go back to Britain of the 1950s where you leave your door open, and there's no cars in the street and every face is exactly the same colour, and, you know, that is not Britain. And it will never happen again.
Errol Drummond

West Bromwich High Street, 2010. Photo: Martin Parr/ Magnum photos

THIS IS IT!
THIS IS IT!
MOST ITEMS 89p
89p
We Unlock
Mobiles

We feel very much at home here but we worry, is it all starting again, this fear of immigrants?

We've just gone through Brexit and, amazingly, some of the conversations that we're having now we've always had. With every new wave of immigrants that comes in we have that and I suppose that will always happen. We have a lot of mis-information.
Errol Drummond

Have we come so far just to see it all happening again? It took us a long time to get here. I never thought I would see integration like it is now. But, now it is here, I am really fearful that it is happening again, like with the Poles. One of them was killed last week, beaten to death.
Hyacinth Jarrett

Right: Wolverhampton market trader, 1990.
Photo: Dave Bagnall
Opposite page:
Miss Pearl, West Bromwich, 2013.
Photo: Martin Parr / Magnum photos

25p
USA 88
99p

Dominoes at the African-Caribbean Resource Centre, West Bromwich. 2016. Photo: Shane Ward

Thinking back

It was just a little kiss on the lips

I went back to Jamaica the other day and I met my first love. I'm thinking if I didn't do what I did at that time, I would be still here and that's the life I would have, that's the life I would be living.

It is so strange when you meet your first love. I was just standing there chatting away and he's standing there looking at me. He came around this side and we were talking and ... I didn't object, I didn't say anything, it was just a little kiss on the lips anyway, and he's just standing there looking at me again, chatting away and it's like you made a friend.

When you grow up there, you don't see all this beauty. We can see now and realise what a beautiful place it is. 'Wow, Jamaica is like that? I left all that and came here?' Yes, I did think about it when I went back and met my first love and I'm thinking, 'Would I be satisfied with that life though?' But then you wouldn't get the experience of what other places are like, what other countries are like. If I go travelling, I do not like to just stay in the hotel. I like to go out a bit to see what the people are like or how things are and what's the difference, because in countries, it's different rules, it's different laws, it's a different culture. Everybody, everywhere it's a different culture so I would like to see what their culture is like, what they're like, and ask questions but if I had stay there, I wouldn't be able to do that.

Annette Simms

St Lucia, 2002.
Photos: Graham Peet

Until death us do part

We are collecting the funeral books of members of the African-Caribbean Resource Centre community who have passed on. We have a lot of them now. We think they show respect for the people who came here, struggled with such difficulties but then managed to become honoured members of this community.

It is like keeping wedding photos. They keep alive the memories of past and present generations as they become a part of the history of their country.
Shane Ward

Above: Funeral books from the African-Caribbean Centre, West Bromwich.
Right: Carmen and Billy Bailey.
Photo from Hyacinth Jarrett

One of the many weddings for which
Hyacinth Jarrett did hairdressing.
Photo from Hyacinth Jarrett

Last words

It makes me feel a bit better, that there's someone there that cares, that wants my opinion. There's not a lot of people that care about our opinion as black youths. So to have someone that comes here to take our information, our opinions to put it in a book, so that the next people can read about it, and see what we're going through. I think that's a great achievement for me.
Oniel Wright

I decided to write my own story down so I can tell my children. I think everyone can do that.
Annette Simms

I am so proud that my father has a place in this book. I have mirrored his journey from the Caribbean to the UK. He will be very pleased to know that our people's stories are being written for our own children to read.
Cllr Jackie Taylor

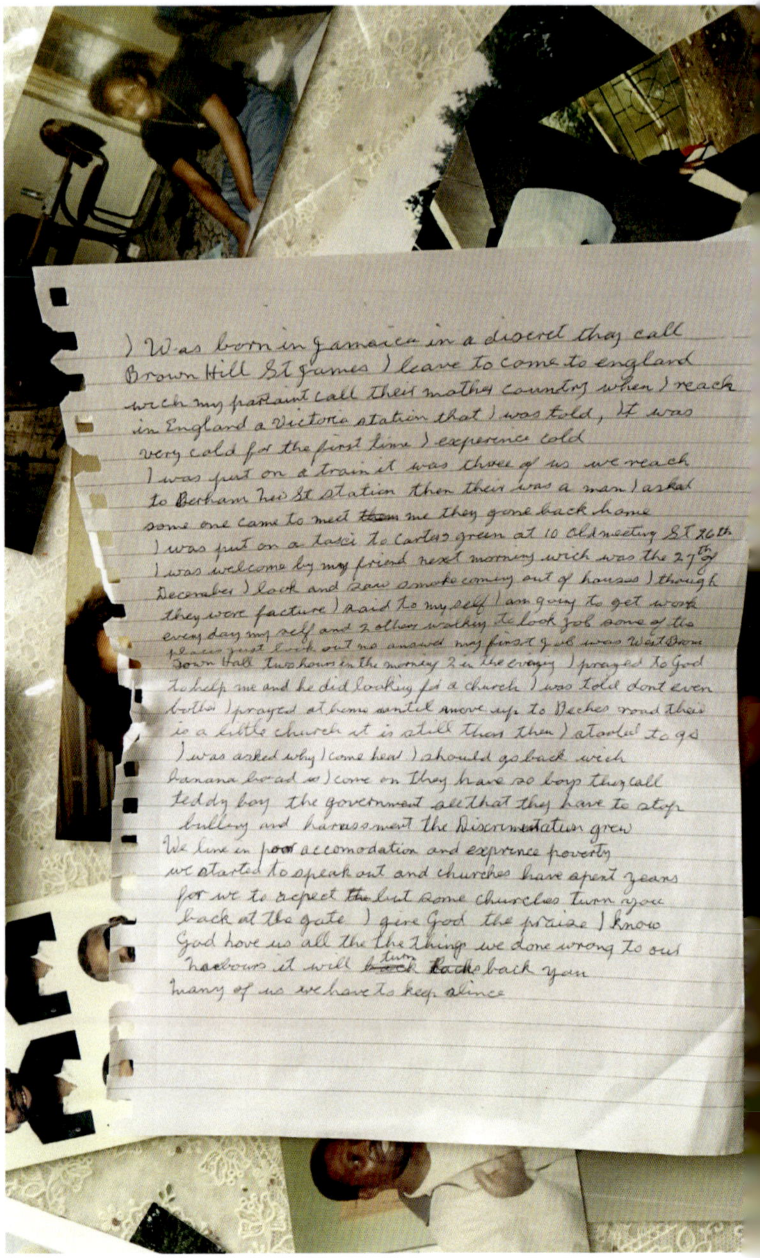

Annette Simms' life story - just the beginning.
Photo: Graham Peet

Cllr Jackie Taylor's father,
Richard Bair,
AKA 'Kingfish'.
From Jamaica to tobacco
fields to West Bromwich in
a life time.
Photos from Jackie Taylor

Credits

Production:

Edited by:
Graham Peet
Emma Purshouse
Kurly McGeachie
Cllr Jackie Taylor
Shane Ward
Hyacinth Jarrett

Interviews:
Emma Purshouse
Kurly McGeachie
Graham Peet

Picture research & design:
Graham Peet

Proof reading:
Caron Wright

Published by: Multistory

Photography:

Nick Hedges, Vanley Burke, Paul Hill, the late Peter Donnelly and all the individuals who loaned their personal photographs.

Martin Parr for photographs by from his series 'Black Country Stories' (2010-2014), commissioned by Multistory.

John Bulmer for photographs from his series 'Black Country', produced for the About Town Magazine, 1961.

Brendan Jackson, Jubilee Arts Archive. www.jubileeartsarchive.com

Sandwell Community History & Archive Service (CHAS).

Assistance:

Many thanks to Cllr Jackie Taylor; the African-Caribbean Resource Centre, West Bromwich; Rachel McFee, OSCAR; Joan Gregory-Bartosch; Simon Meddings; Gemma Hadley for additional transcription; Dave Hughes for additional proof reading.

All cover photos credited in the text except bottom right: Daniel Forbes.

ISBN 978-0-9955062-1-3

Supported using public funding by ARTS COUNCIL ENGLAND

Light and colour
We see colours when light shines on things. It is hard to make out colours in the dark, as very little light is reflected from them into our eyes.

PRINCIPLES OF LIGHT

What is light?
We see when light reflects off things into our eyes. Light is a form of energy called electromagnetic radiation, made up of electrically charged particles. The total spectrum of radiation includes X-rays, ultra violet rays, infra red and radio waves. They each have a different wavelength, or speed of vibration (frequency). Our eyes only react to a very small group of wavelengths that makes visible light.

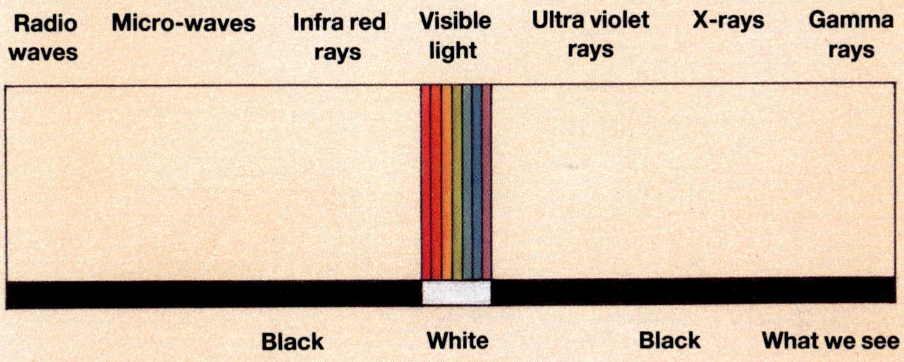

The Sun's energy
Light from the Sun is a mixture of seven colours that we see as white light. Huge amounts of heat and light energy are produced from nuclear reactions deep inside the Sun. Temperatures on the surface can reach 6000 degrees Celsius (°C).

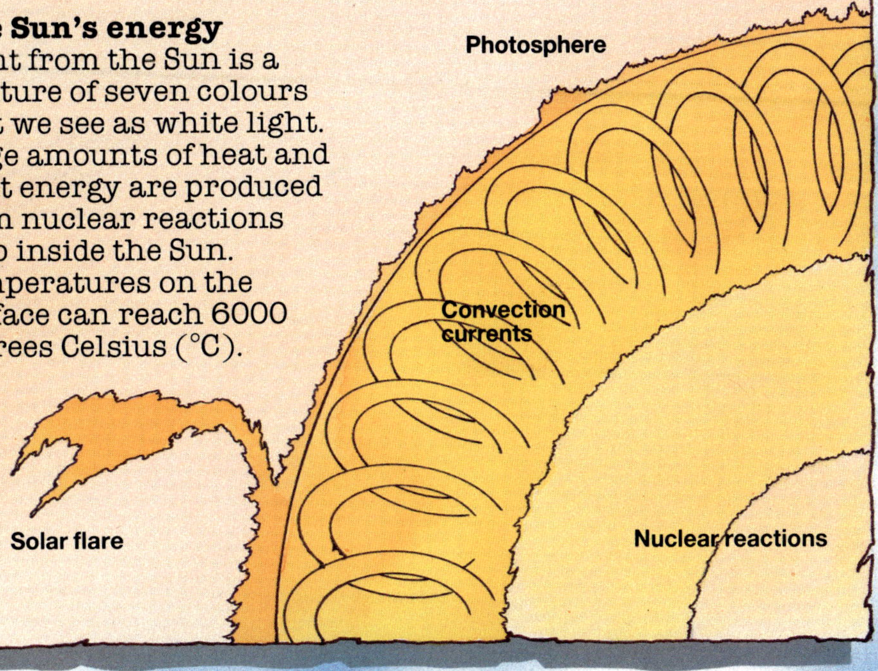

MAKE YOUR OWN SUNDIAL

Set up your sundial on a window sill in a south-facing room early in the morning. You will need a watch and a pen. When your watch shows a whole hour (like 8 a.m.), draw a line passing through the centre of the pencil's shadow and write the time beside it. Do this every hour, on the hour, until late into the afternoon. Notice how the length of the shadow changes during the day.

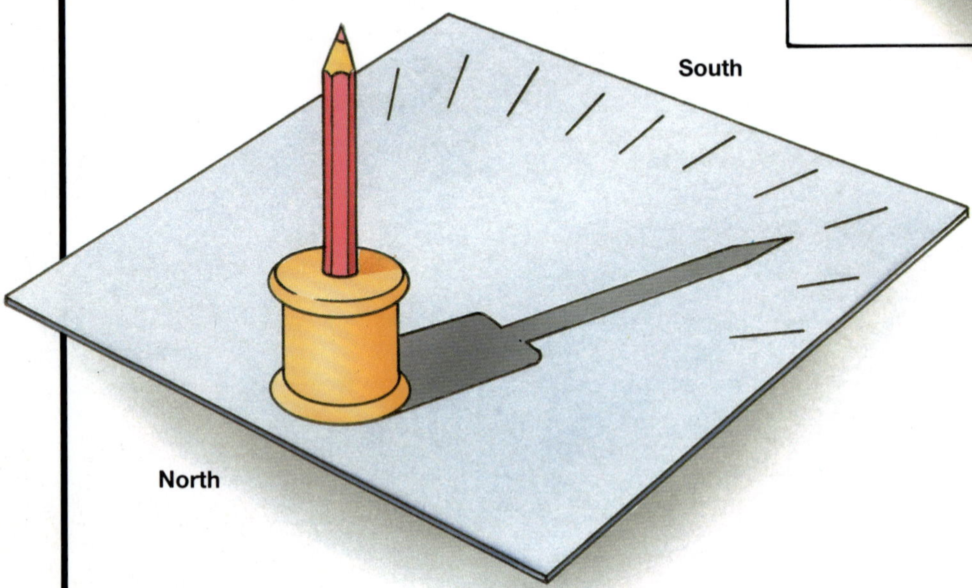

Any shadow lines missed because the Sun was hidden by cloud can be added on another day. Once marked with the hours, your sundial will show the time whenever the Sun shines.

HOW TALL IS THAT TREE?

You can find the height of a tree with a metre-long stick and shadows. Use the stick to measure the length of the tree's shadow, to the nearest metre. Measure the stick's shadow to the nearest decimetre. Use a calculator to divide the length of the tree's shadow by the length of the stick's shadow to give the tree's height. If a tree's shadow is 12 metres and the stick's shadow is 1.5 metres, the tree's height is 8 metres (12 divided by 1.5).

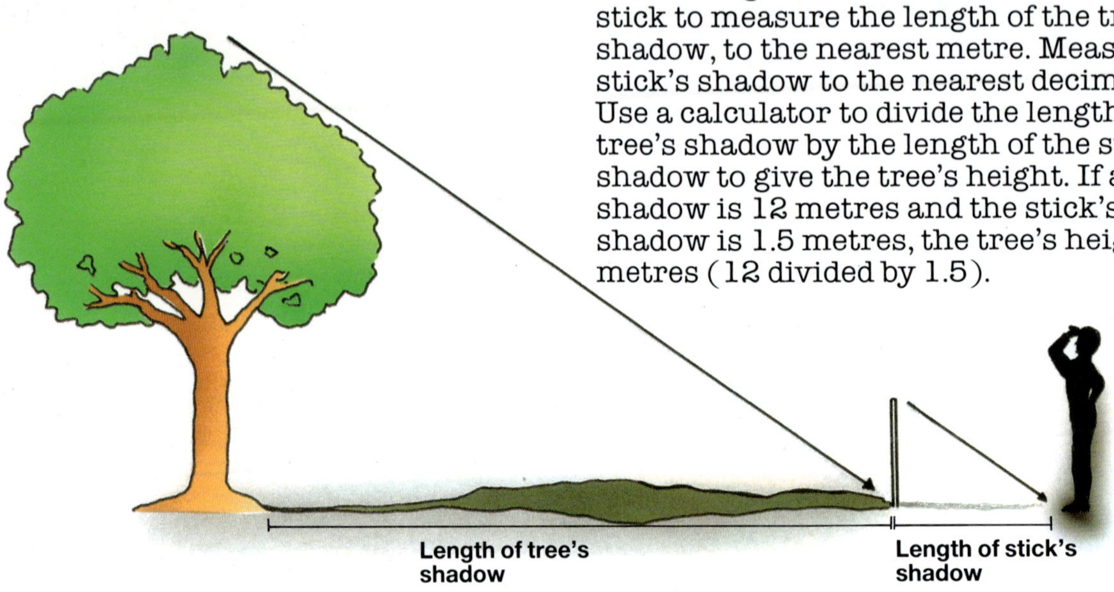

PLAYING WITH SHADOWS

Look for your shadow on a bright, sunny day. Can you run away and leave it behind? Shadow box with a friend's shadow, without touching each other. Use a torch or table lamp in a dark room to make shadows on a wall. Watch what happens to their size if you move things towards or away from the light.

Hand shadows
Try making animal shapes with your hands, like a bird that flaps its wings. Use your finger tips to make the head of a dog.

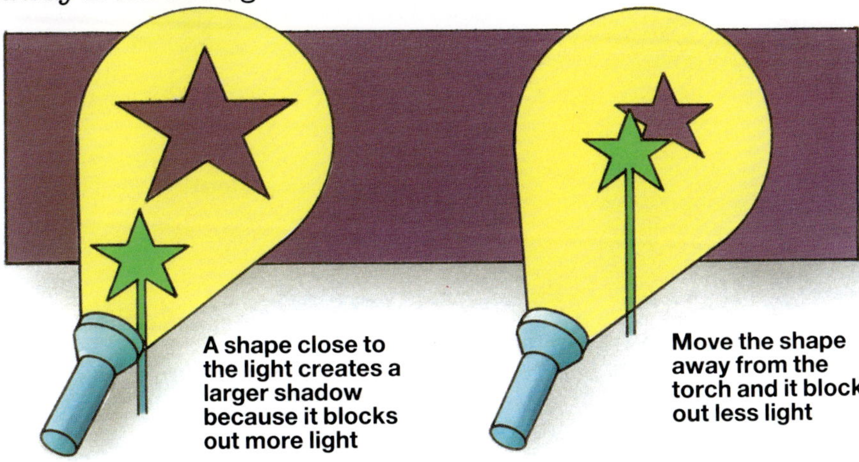

SHADOW PUPPET THEATRE

Use a lamp to light up a screen made from an old cotton sheet or table cloth. Carefully cut out scenery and character shapes from card. Pin the scenery to the sheet. Tape your characters to thin sticks, like garden canes, so they can move across the screen. Make up a play to entertain your friends and family. You can make your shadow puppets even more realistic by having moving parts held together with paper fasteners.

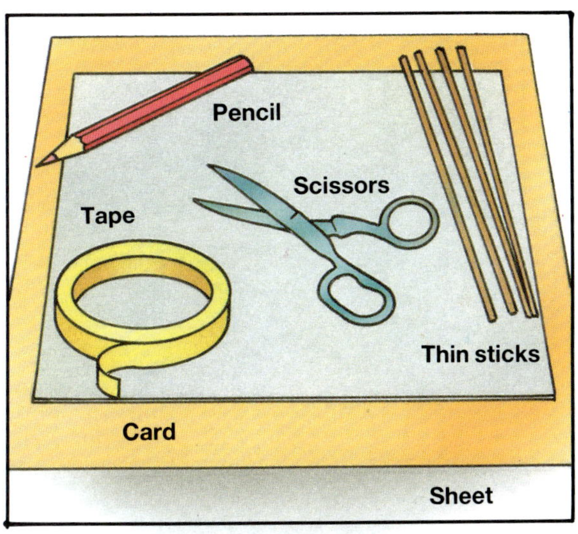

LIGHT TRAVELS IN STRAIGHT LINES

You can show that light travels in a straight line if you put a tiny light, like a small bulb or a candle, at one end of a table. (Stand a candle in a tray full of sand or set securely on a saucer.) Make a small hole in a square of card and set the card in modelling clay so that you can see the light through the hole. Line up the hole in a second card so that you can still see the bulb or flame. Set up a third card, too, so that you can see the light through all three holes. Always blow out the candle after your investigation.

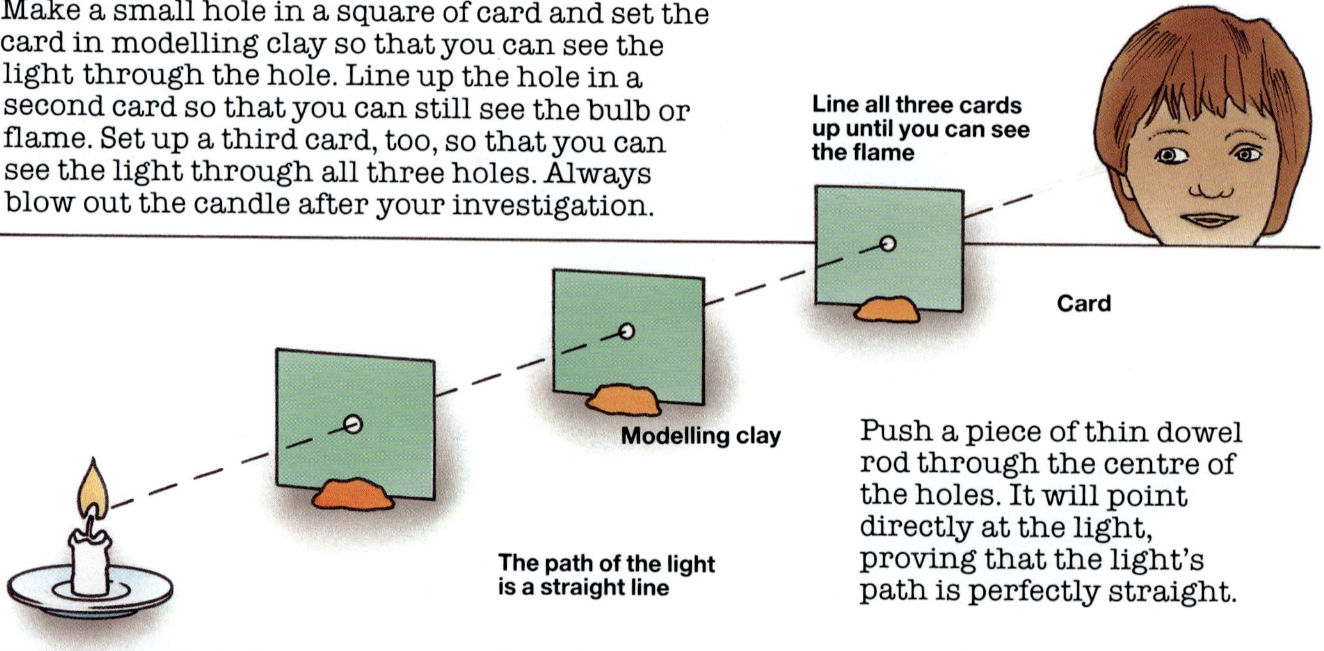

Push a piece of thin dowel rod through the centre of the holes. It will point directly at the light, proving that the light's path is perfectly straight.

MAKE YOUR OWN LIGHT-RAY BOX

Many interesting experiments can be done using a light box. The light from a torch shines through the slit in the box. Put your light box on a table in a darkened room and set a mirror in front of it. Watch how the angle between the light beam and its reflection changes as you move the mirror.

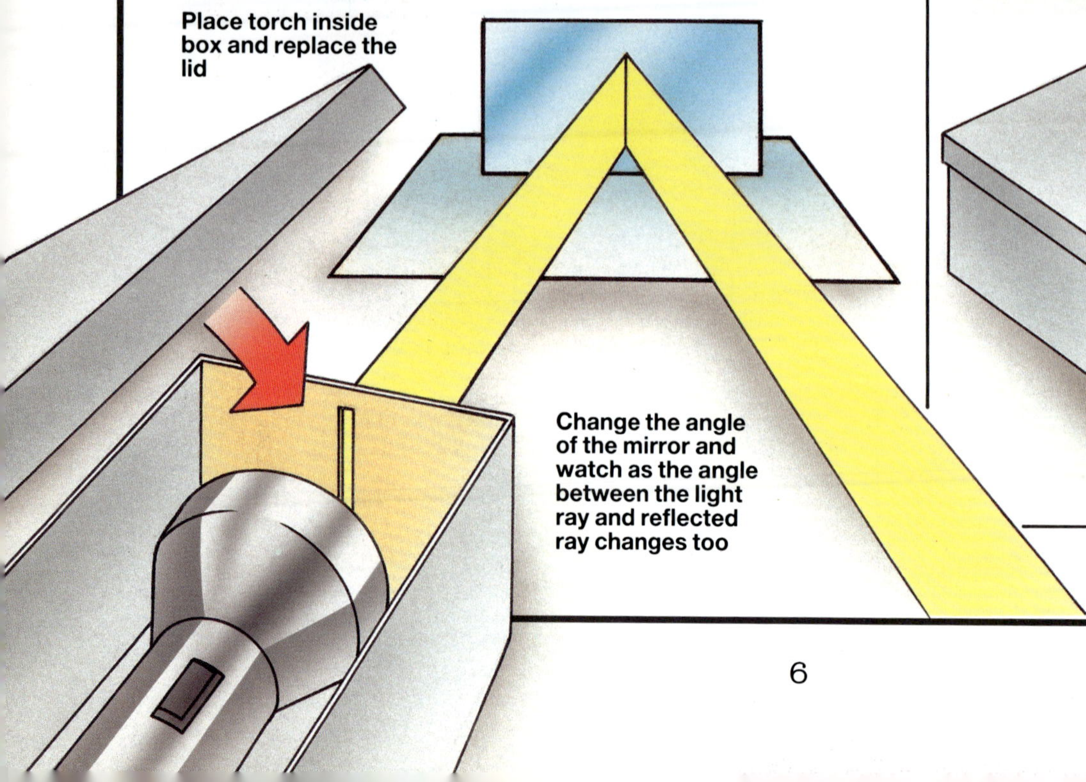

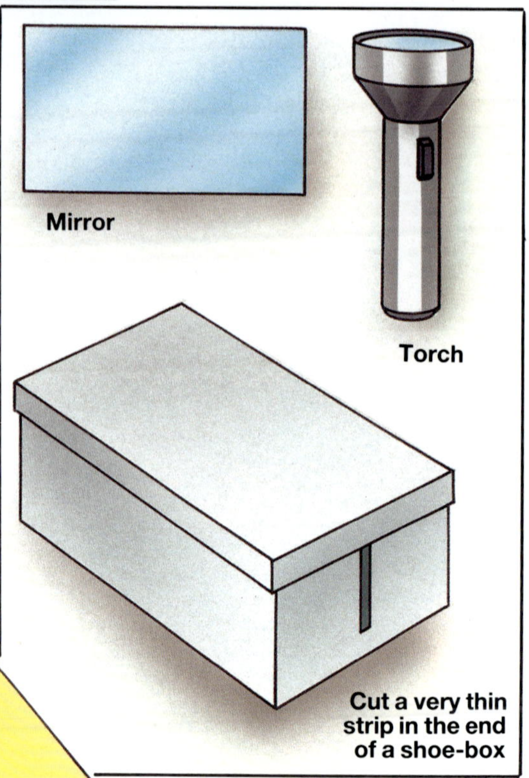

MAKE YOUR OWN PERISCOPE

Can you see round a corner or over a wall without being seen? Submarines use periscopes to see what is above them without having to come to the surface. You can make a periscope from card with slits cut into the sides to take two small mirrors. You must set the angle of the mirror slits at 45° (half a right angle), so that the light will be reflected through the periscope tube.

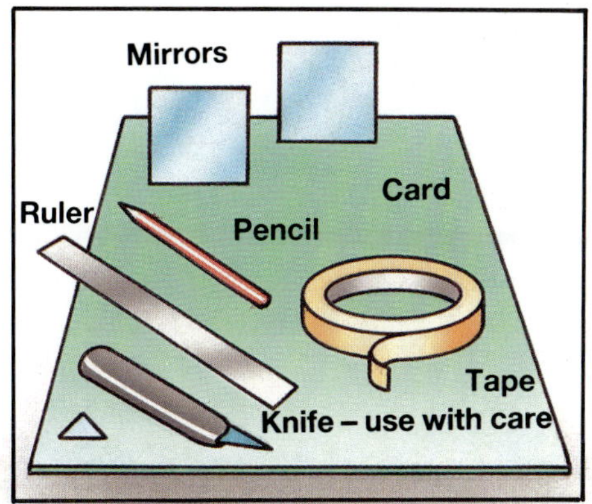

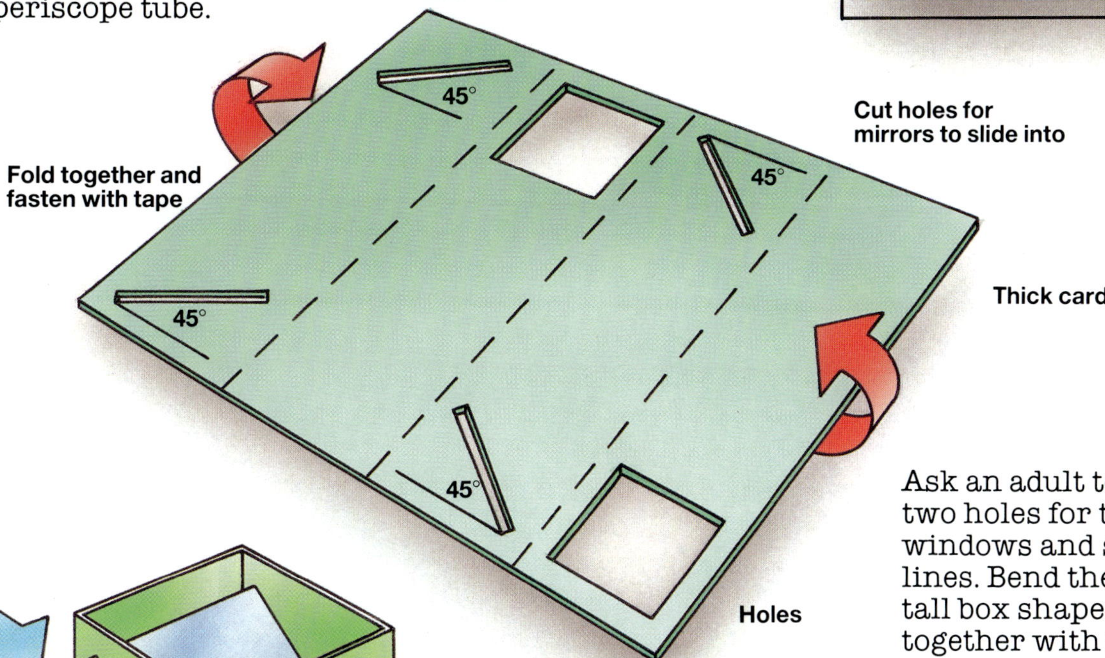

Ask an adult to cut out the two holes for the viewing windows and score the fold lines. Bend the card into a tall box shape. Hold it together with tape.

How it works
Light, reflected from an object, enters through the top window and is reflected off the top mirror. The angle of the mirror sends the light down to the bottom mirror. This reflects the light out through the bottom window and into your eyes.

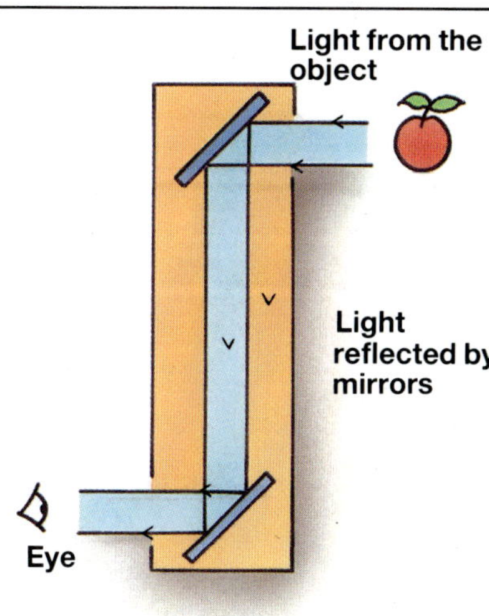

MAKE YOUR OWN KALEIDOSCOPE

Kaleidoscopes are very old toys that use mirrors to produce colourful, changing patterns. You can make your own by taping together three small mirrors into a triangle. Hold the mirrors over a collection of small beads or brightly coloured tissue paper scraps and look down inside the mirrors. To change the pattern, find a transparent dish or jar that the mirrors can stand in. Hold the dish and the mirrors up, so that light can shine in through the bottom, and slowly turn the dish as you look down. The effect is even better if you can hold your kaleidoscope at an angle so that the beads move inside the mirrors.

Multiple reflections

Tape two small mirrors together and stand them on a table top. Place a small toy between them and count the number of reflections that you can see. Make the angle larger, by moving the mirrors apart. Is the number of reflections more or less? Now move the mirrors closer together. Watch what happens to the number of reflections.

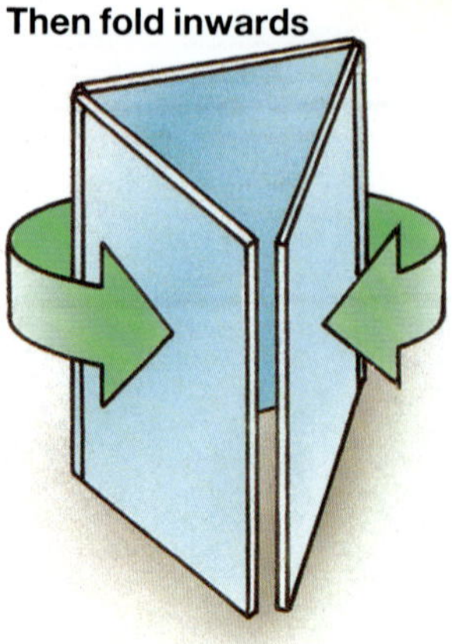

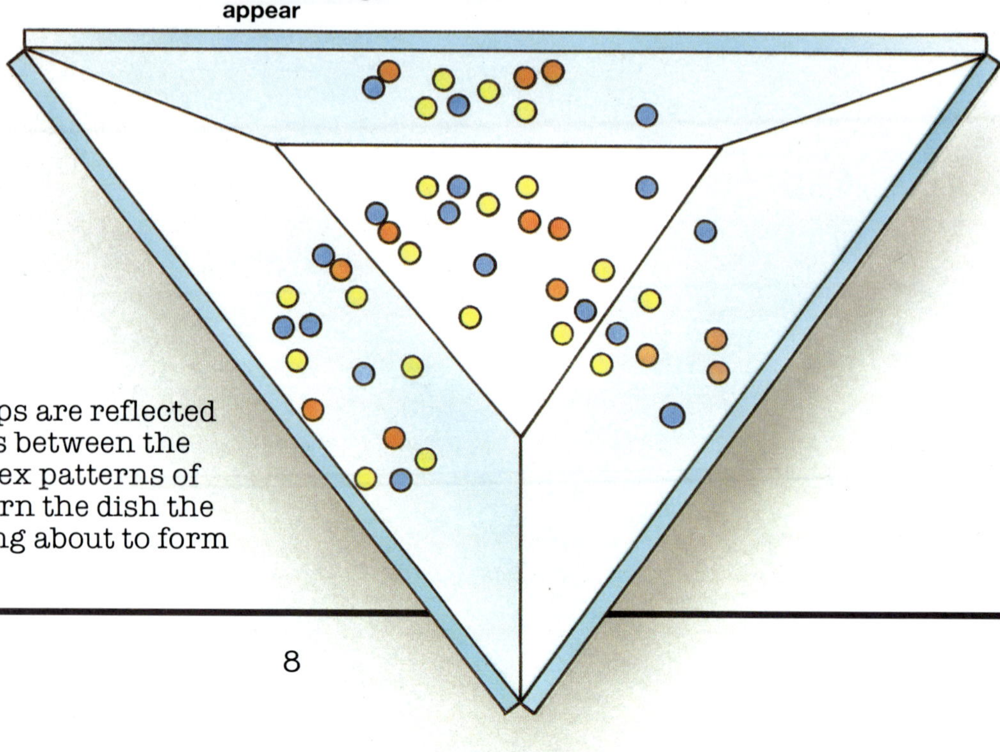

The beads or tissue scraps are reflected backwards and forwards between the mirrors, building complex patterns of coloured light. As you turn the dish the beads roll around, moving about to form new patterns.

SPOON MIRRORS

Have you ever been to a fairground hall of mirrors? The strangely shaped mirrors make you look very odd indeed. Any bendy mirror will distort or alter your shape. You may be lucky enough to have a plastic mirror that you can bend gently to change to the shape of your reflection. If not, you can use a large spoon. Look into the bowl of a very shiny spoon. This is like a concave or hollowed out mirror. What is strange about your image? Now turn the spoon around and look at your reflection in the back of the spoon. This is a convex mirror. How do you look now?

Convex – the back of the spoon makes the image the right way up

Concave – the bowl of the spoon makes the image appear upside down

MYSTERY MONEY

If you look at fish in a pool they seem quite close. When you dip your hand in to touch them you find they are deeper than you thought. Your eyes are being fooled by an illusion created by the water. Light rays bend as they pass from water into air and make you think that the water is shallower than it really is.

Bendy pencil
Light rays change direction as they pass from water to air, so any object in water seems to bend. A pencil seems to be bent at the place where it enters the water.

Put a coin in a bowl. Look over the rim, slowly bend down until the coin disappears from view. Get someone to pour water slowly into the bowl. As it fills the coin will reappear.

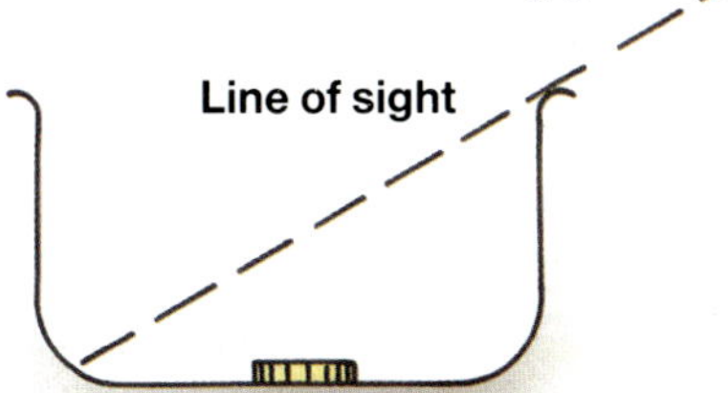

The light reflected from the coin is bent towards you as it passes from the water into the air. So you can now see the coin, even though the rim hid it before.

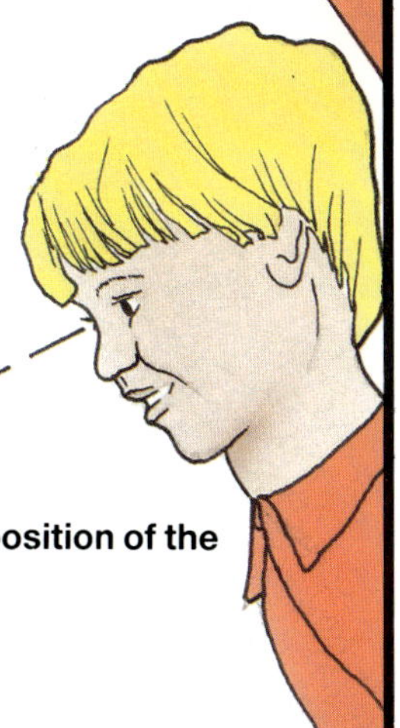

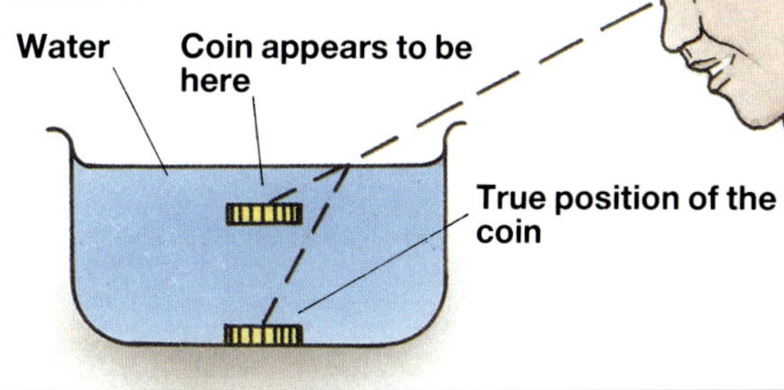

NEAR AND FAR

Lenses bend or refract light, changing the image that we see. Someone who finds it hard to see objects close up (this is called being long-sighted), wears glasses fitted with convex or magnifying lenses to re-focus the light onto the retina at the back of the eyes. People who cannot focus on far-off objects (they are short-sighted), wear glasses with concave lenses. You can see the effects of these different lenses by holding them in the path of a series of light rays shining through slots cut into the end of a shoe-box. Set up the light box in a darkened room and observe how the light rays are bent, or refracted, through the lenses.

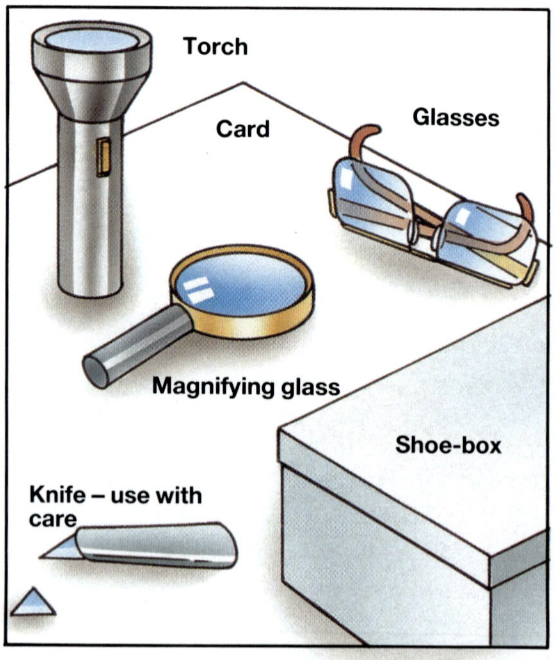

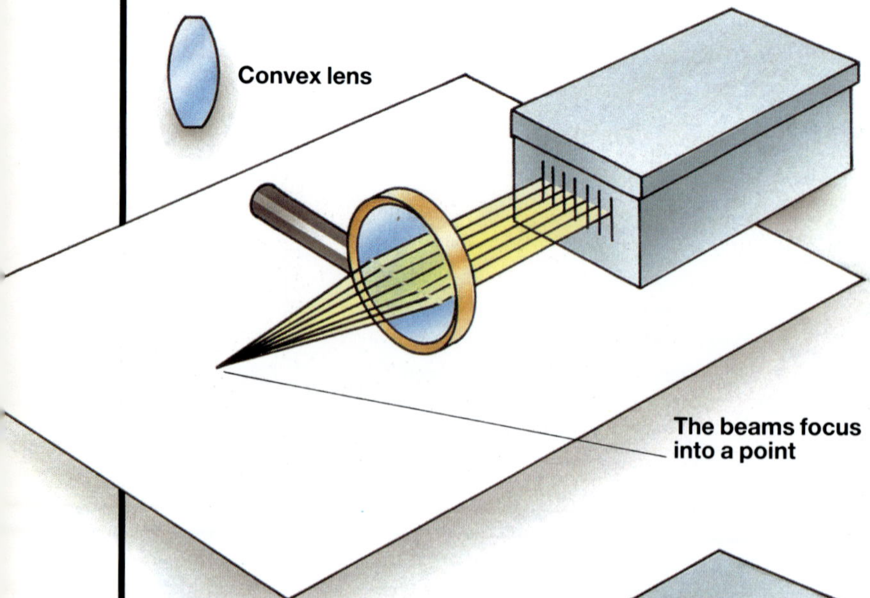

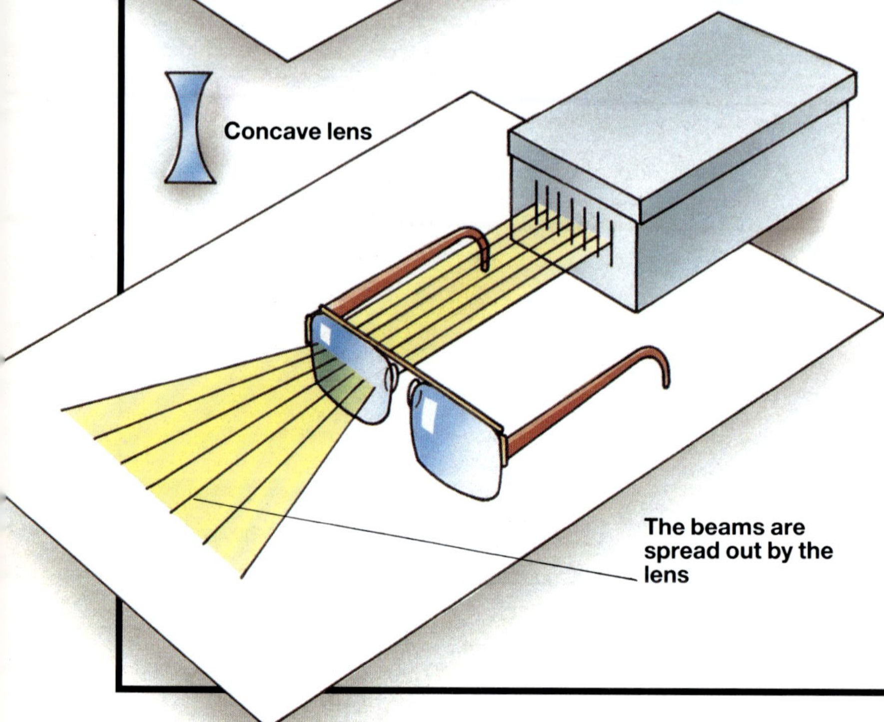

Water drop lens
Water has a "skin" caused by tension in the surface that pulls small drops of water into a rounded shape. Because of this, water drops can act like tiny convex lenses. Put a drop of water on a thin piece of transparent plastic or glass and place it on a picture. You will see the picture seems to be much bigger.

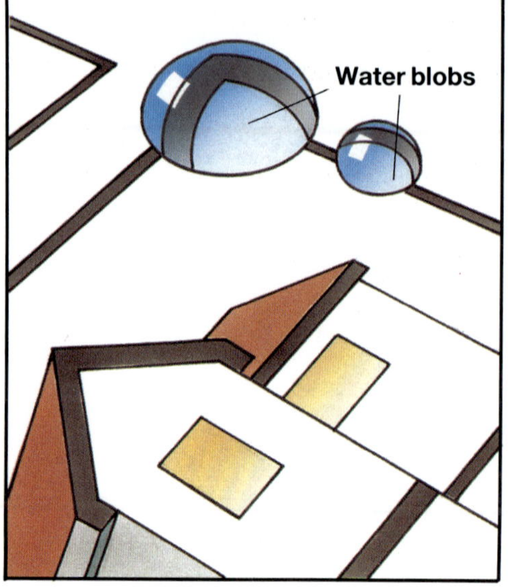

TELESCOPES

People have known for at least 800 years that lenses can magnify objects. The earliest telescopes were made by Flemish lens grinders. These early refracting telescopes (telescopes that use glass lenses to magnify and focus light) did not magnify things very well but an Italian scientist and astronomer named Galileo showed how they could be improved to allow very detailed observations to be made. Reflecting telescopes, invented by the English scientist, Newton, used a concave mirror to collect light from distant objects. As mirrors were easier to make, his reflecting telescopes could be made much larger; which led to further discoveries. Even the radio waves that are produced by distant stars and galaxies can be collected and focused by special dishes that make up radio telescopes. These give valuable information about objects at the very edge of the universe.

Refracting telescopes

A simple refracting telescope can be made with two convex lenses in a tube. More powerful refracting telescopes use many lenses, giving a clearer, sharper image.

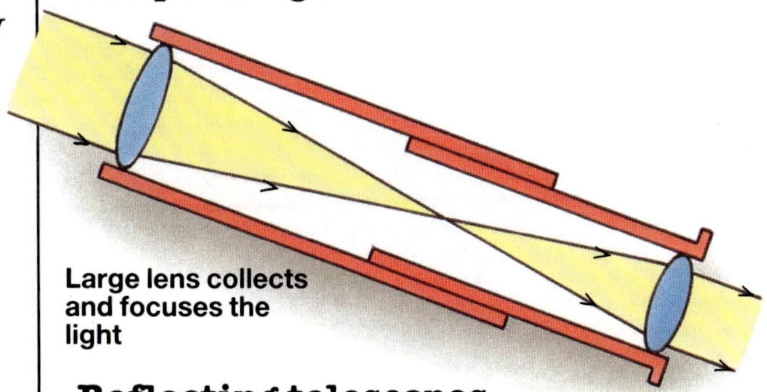

Reflecting telescopes

Instead of a lens, reflecting telescopes use a concave mirror to collect and focus the light. An eyepiece lens increases the magnification of the image.

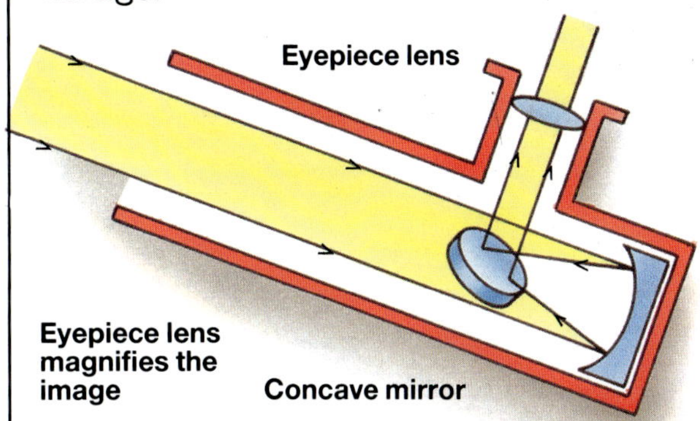

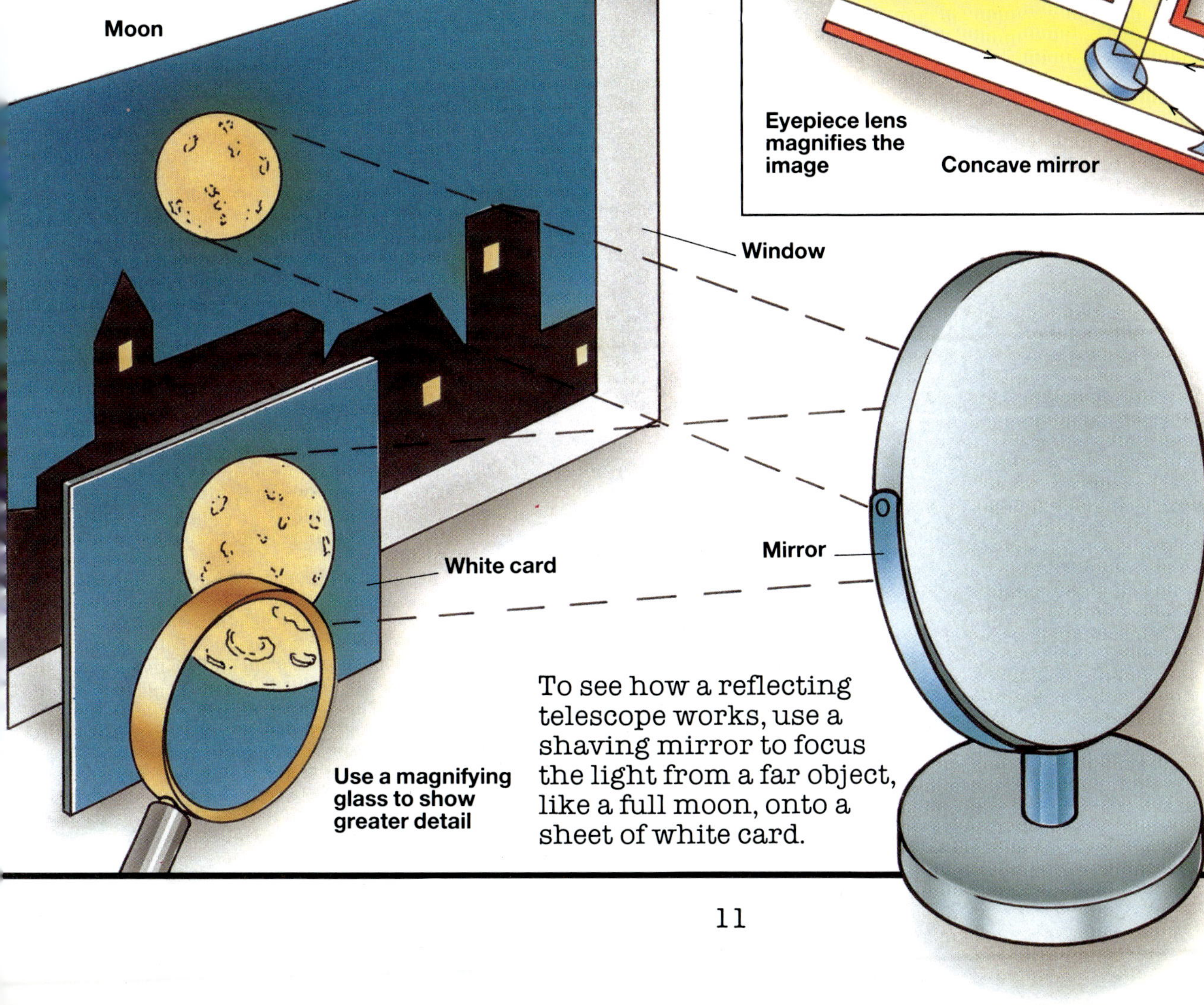

To see how a reflecting telescope works, use a shaving mirror to focus the light from a far object, like a full moon, onto a sheet of white card.

SPLITTING WHITE LIGHT

White light, the light that comes from the Sun, can be split into seven different colours, called the spectrum of visible light, using a glass prism. A ray of light refracted through the glass is divided up into these seven colours because each colour has a different wavelength and so it is bent or refracted through a different angle. The colours are red, orange, yellow, blue, green, indigo and violet.

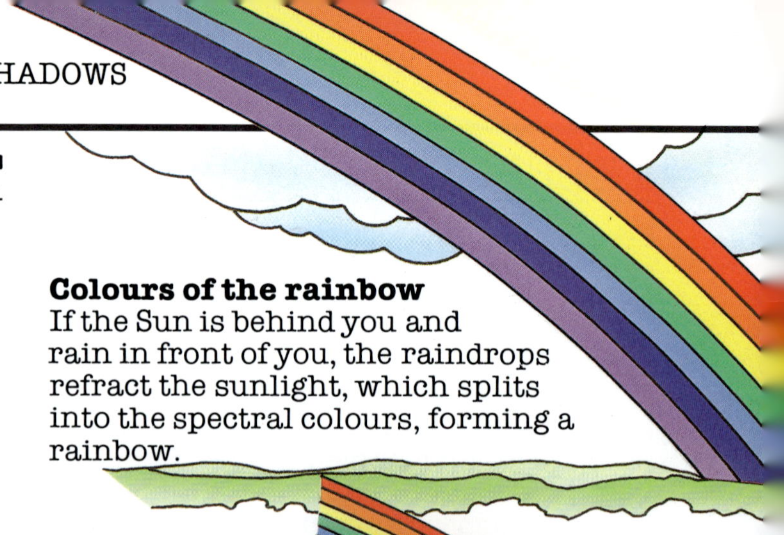

Colours of the rainbow
If the Sun is behind you and rain in front of you, the raindrops refract the sunlight, which splits into the spectral colours, forming a rainbow.

Sir Isaac Newton
In 1666 Newton discovered that white light is made up of different colours. He used a prism to split a beam of sunlight coming through a slit in a window blind into a darkened room.

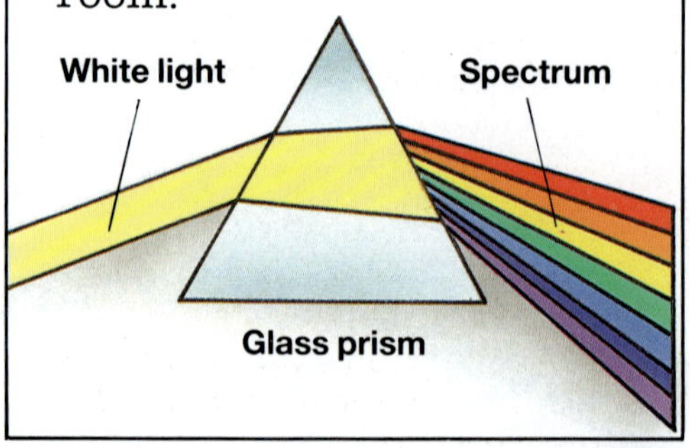

Hose pipe rainbow
On a sunny day, adjust the nozzle on a hose pipe to make a fine mist of water. Stand with your back to the Sun and spray the water into the air. You will see a rainbow in the mist of water droplets.

COLOUR SPINNERS

Mixing light is very different from mixing paint. The more colours of paints or pigments that are mixed together, the darker the mixture becomes. This is called subtractive colour mixing. When light of different colours is mixed, the lighter it becomes. This is called additive colour mixing. Light reflected from colour spinners mixes in this way. To see this for yourself, use a cup to draw circles on pieces of white card and carefully cut these out. Push a pencil stub through the centre of each spinner disc. (Short pencil stubs are easier to spin.) Colour the discs with paints or felt-tipped pens, dividing each disc into seven equal areas and colouring each area with a different colour of the spectrum. Then set the discs spinning.

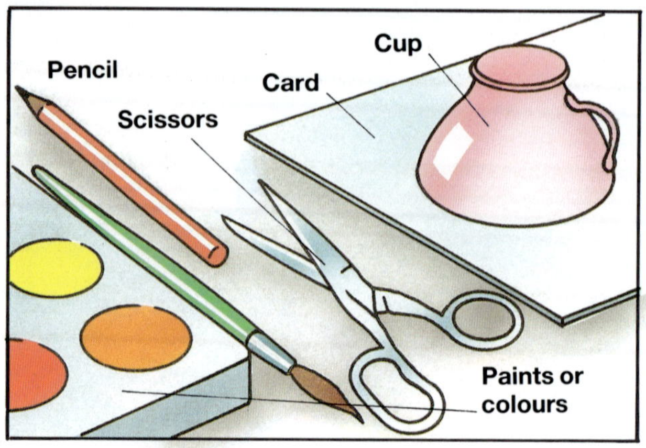

Use cup to draw circle on card and cut out

MAKE YOUR OWN SPECTRUM

Carefully cut a slit into a sheet of card and tape it to a window. Darken the room by pulling the curtains or blinds, letting through only the ray of light from the slit. Reflect the light ray from a mirror lying in a dish of water onto a piece of white card.

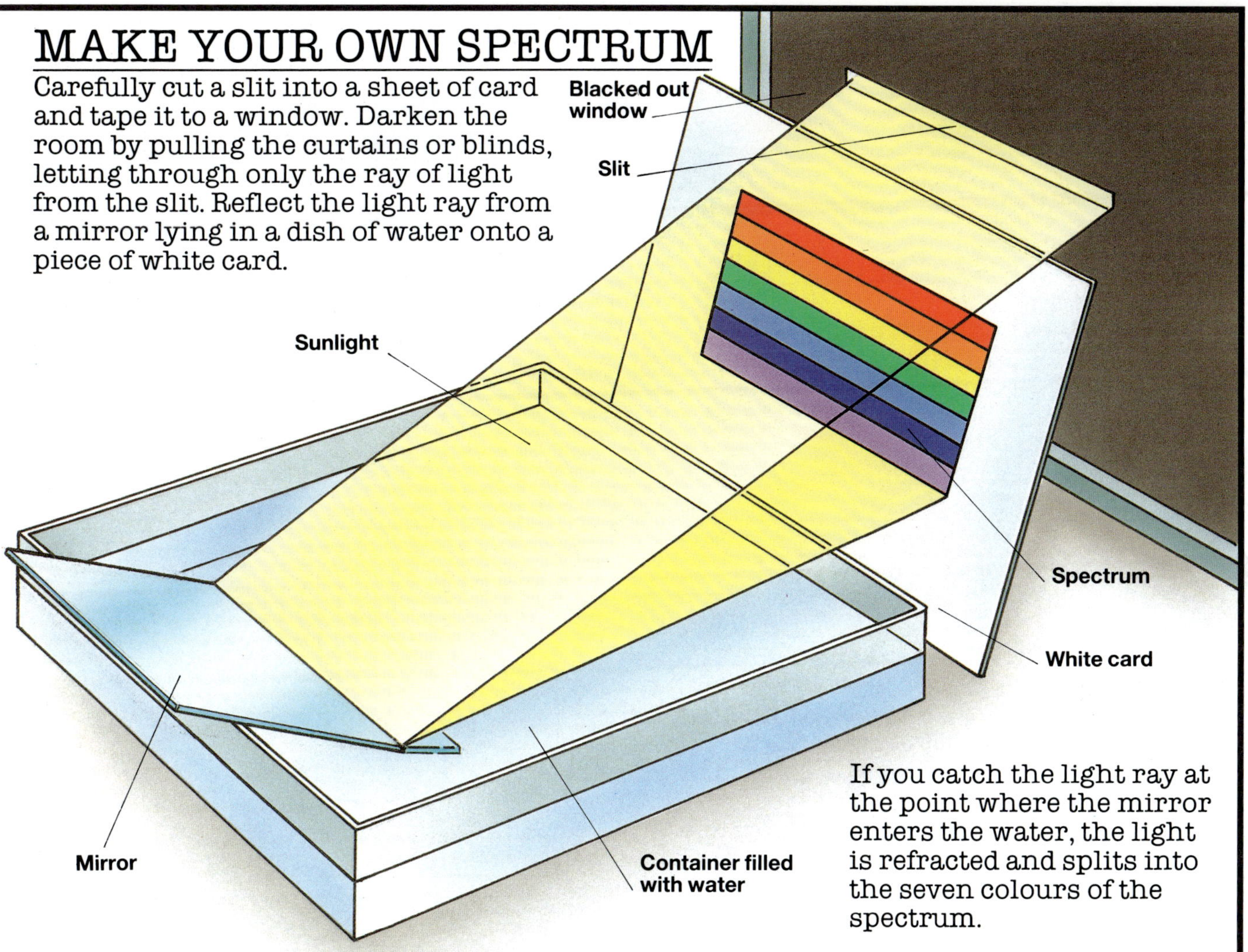

If you catch the light ray at the point where the mirror enters the water, the light is refracted and splits into the seven colours of the spectrum.

You can test the effect of different colour combinations on different spinners.

Because the disc spins so quickly your eyes cannot make out the separate colours and they merge together so that the disc looks grey/white. You can never get a perfect white because the card and paints are not pure colours.

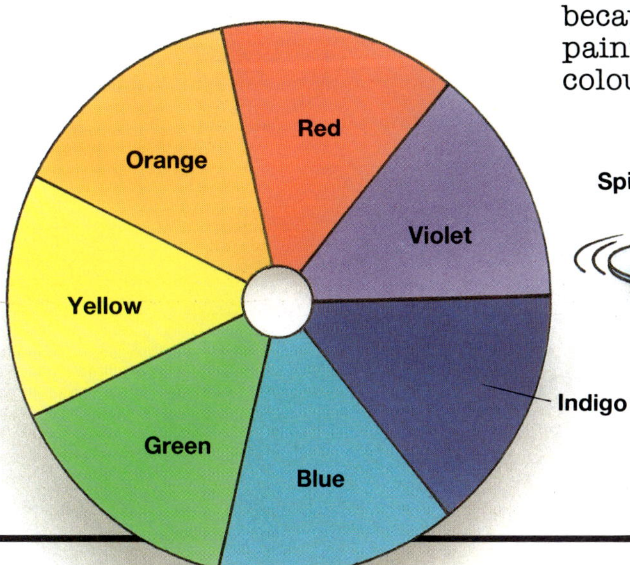

Why we see colour
We see colours because everything around us absorbs white light and reflects back only some of the spectral colours. White objects reflect almost all the spectrum, but black ones absorb them, reflecting back almost no colour at all. Red things absorb spectral colours, reflecting only red light. Blue objects reflect blue light, and so on.

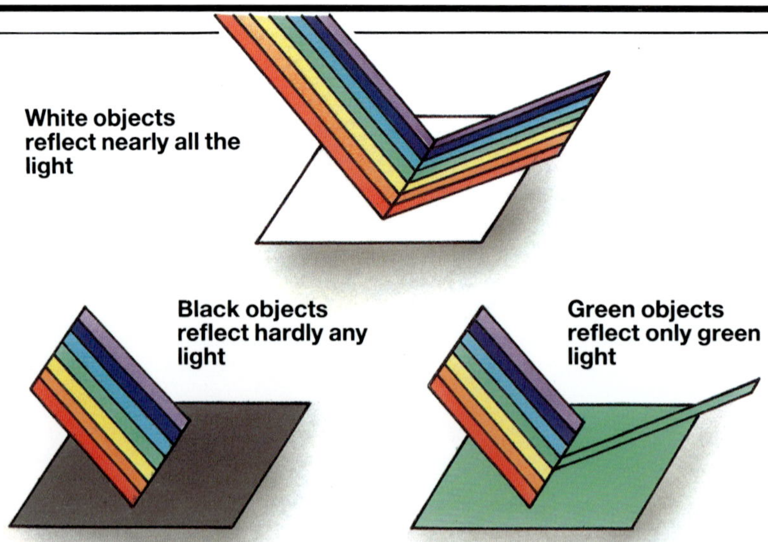

MIXING WITH LIGHT

You can see what happens when coloured light is shone on objects. Ask friends to help you with this experiment. Cover three powerful torches with red, blue and green cellophane or colour filters. Shine all three torches on a sheet of white paper in a very dark room. Look carefully at the way light mixes, it is not like mixing paint. Paints mix to make darker colours, light mixes to make lighter colours. Notice how the colour of objects like your toys changes when you shine coloured light on them.

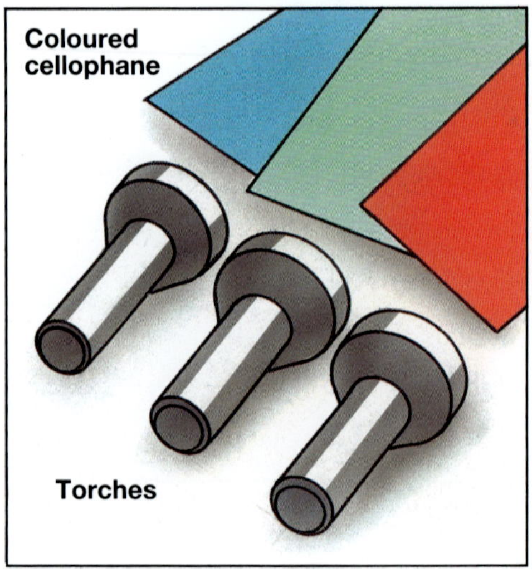

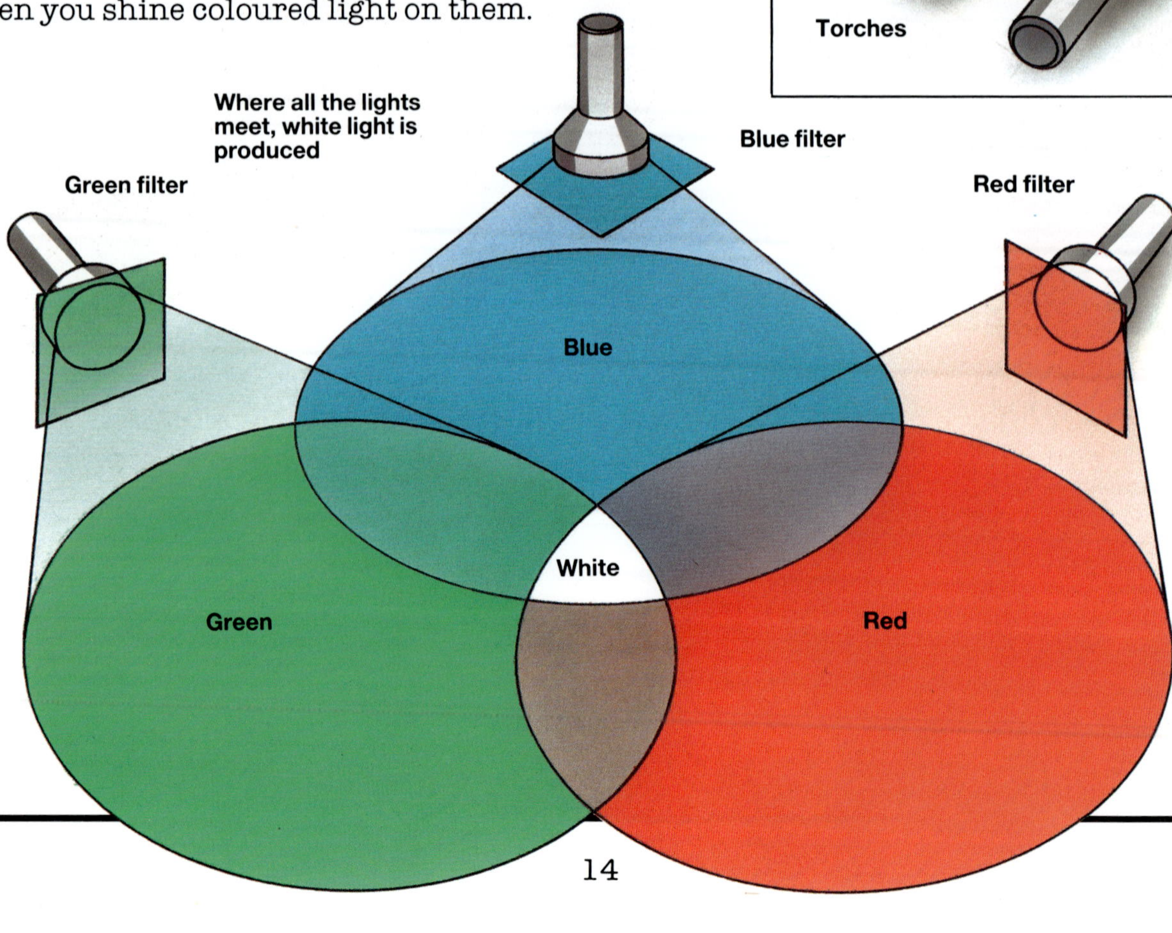

SEPARATING COLOURS

Many colours, such as food dyes and the ink in felt-tipped pens, are mixtures of colours. It is possible to split some colours by a process called chromatography. Put a large spot of one colour at the bottom of a strip of blotting paper. Tape the strip to a pencil and rest it on a jar with some water in it. The water soaks into the blotting paper, carrying the ink with it. The different colours in the ink move at different speeds, so they spread out along the paper.

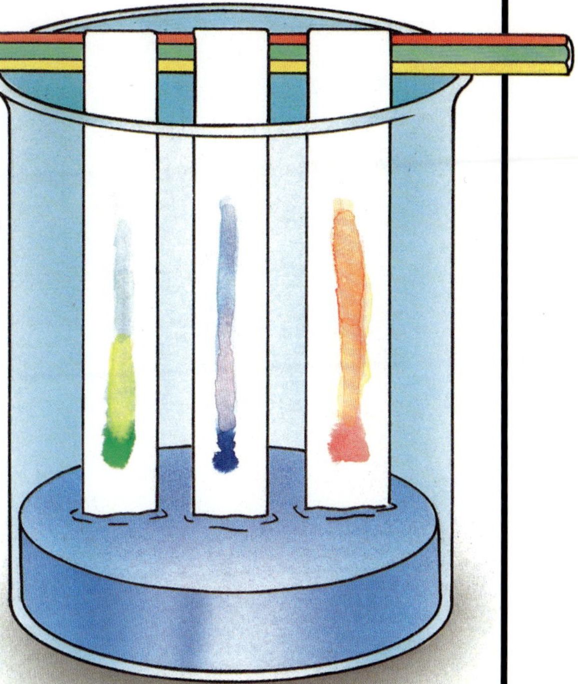

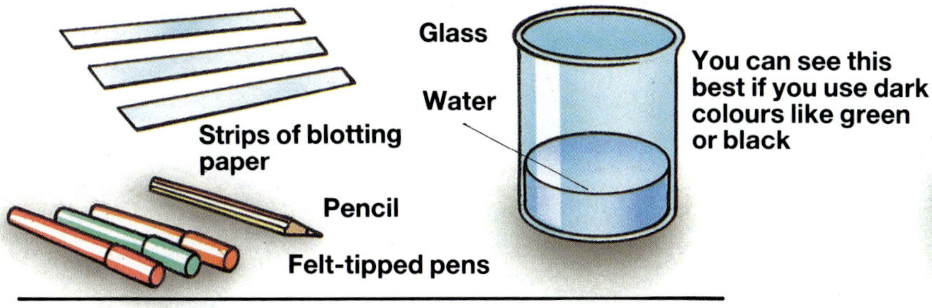

SEEING RED

Carefully cut out some card glasses at about the size shown. Find some pieces of coloured cellophane, like sweet wrappers. Any coloured material that you can see through clearly will do. Paste the pieces over the eye holes of your glasses and look at familiar objects. Notice how their colours are changed. Try different coloured cellophane in your glasses. Do you like a yellow world or would you prefer a cool blue one? Do some colours make you feel warm, do others make you happy? Which is your favourite colour?

CHEMICAL ENERGY

Chemical energy is a form of stored energy or fuel. Most chemical energy is released by burning, giving heat and light. Fuel liko oil, gas and coal was formed over millions of years from dead plants and animals. Food is also stored energy. Plants make their own food from sunlight by a process called photosynthesis. Some animals (herbivores) eat plants to get the energy they need to grow. Other animals (carnivores) get their food energy by eating other animals.

Why do we eat?
We eat to get energy. Food is broken down inside our bodies into proteins, vitamins, minerals and so on. This is digestion. It provides all the things we need to keep warm, to grow and to stay healthy.

Solar energy
The Sun gives us all the energy we need, but we cannot live off warmth and sunlight alone. We need food. The Sun makes our food, which gives us our energy.

PRINCIPLES OF CHEMICAL ENERGY

Food chains
Herbivores are animals that eat plants to get the energy they need to live. Other animals, the carnivores, eat the herbivores. When animals die, scavengers such as insects eat the dead tissue. Dead plant material, such as leaf mould and tree bark, forms the food of many fungi. Decayed plant and animal tissue produces minerals to fertilize the land for more plants to grow. Everywhere there are complex food chains of plants and animals living off each other. Each link in the chain gets the energy it needs for life from other plants or animals. Every food chain begins with green plants and the Sun.

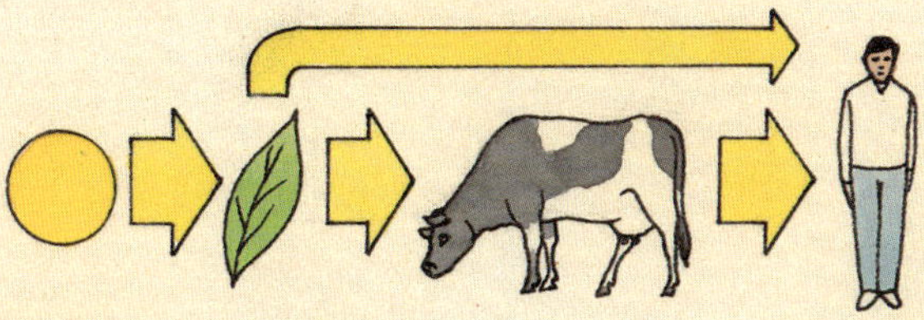

The food chain

Oxygen and carbon dioxide
The chemical energy in food that is essential for life can only be released in the body's cells if oxygen is present there as well. All animals need a constant supply of oxygen, breathed in from the air, so that a complex series of chemical reactions can take place to release the energy. Animals breathe out carbon dioxide as a waste product (something they do not need) of these reactions. Plants take in carbon dioxide, from the air or absorbed in water, to create their own energy. They give out oxygen as a product of photosynthesis, putting the oxygen which animals need back into the atmosphere.

Animals and plants
Animals depend upon plants for their food energy. Animals are energy-consumers; plants are energy-producers, but where do plants get their energy supply?

Photosynthesis
Green plants make energy through a process called photosynthesis. Complex chemical reactions turn carbon dioxide, water and sunlight into energy-rich sugars and oxygen, using a chemical, chlorophyll, that gives leaves their green colour.

CANDLE SNUFFER

A candle burns until its wax has gone, unless it is blown out. It gets its chemical energy from the wax. But it also needs air to make it burn. Put a candle in a tray of sand or soil and ask an adult to light it for you. Put a large glass (not plastic) jar over the candle. When the candle has used up the air in the jar it goes out.

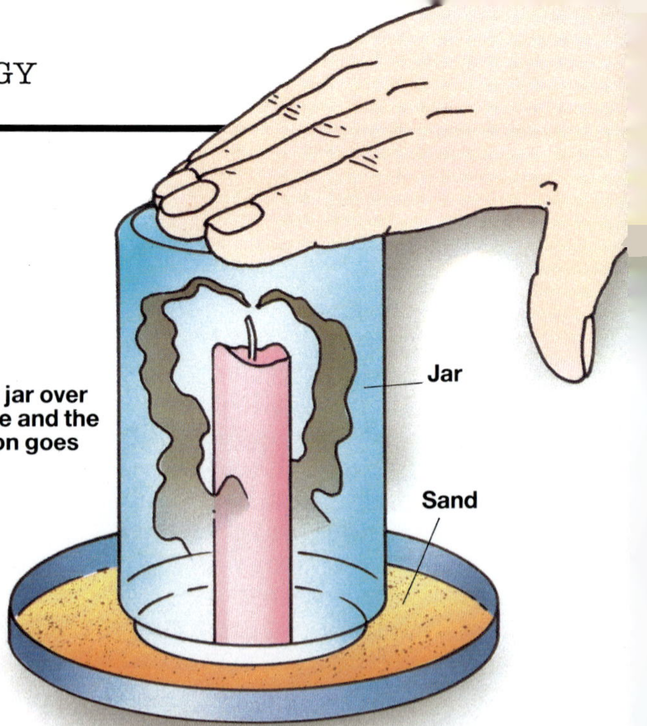

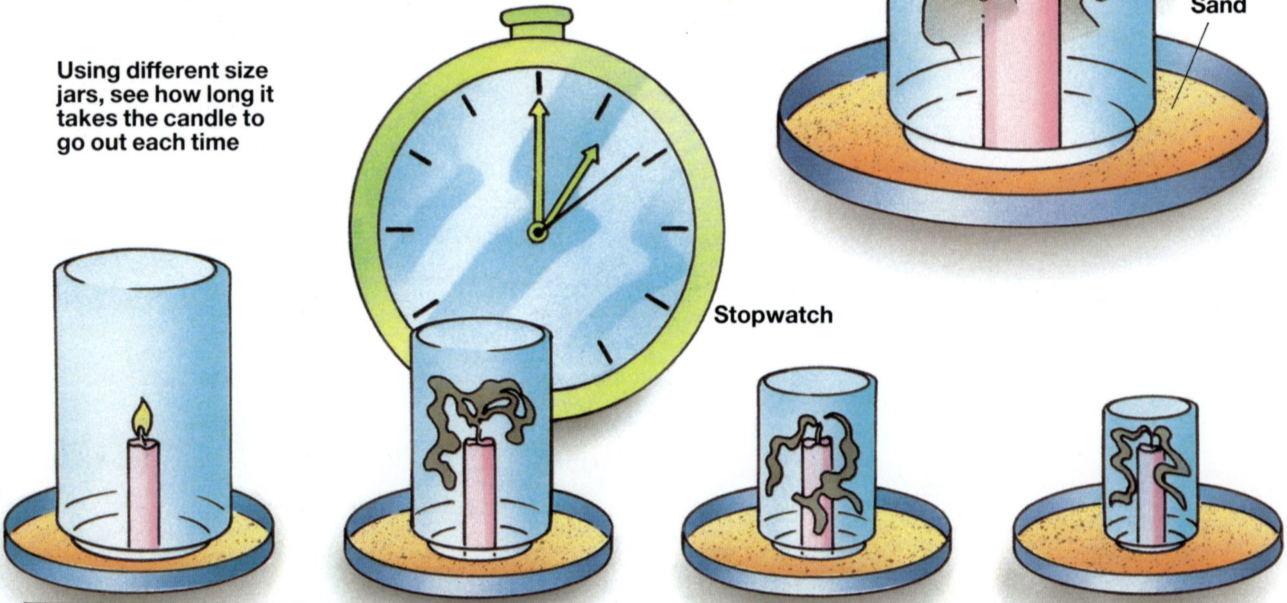

DOES ALL AIR BURN?

Put a candle in a dish of water. Ask an adult to light it. Put a glass jar over it, resting on some coins to keep a gap between the jar and dish. As the candle burns, it uses up part of the air in the jar. The space left by the used up air is filled by water sucked in from the dish, but it only fills about a fifth of the space in the jar.

Air is about four fifths nitrogen, one fifth oxygen, with a tiny amount of carbon dioxide and other gases. Only oxygen burns, so it is the space left by that which is filled by the water.

FIRE-FIGHTING

To put out a fire you must stop oxygen reaching it. Water will drench the fire, so air can't reach it, fire-proof blankets can be thrown over small fires, and foam or carbon dioxide extinguishers will smother a fire in the same way. You can make your own carbon dioxide extinguisher with bicarbonate of soda (baking powder) and vinegar. The baking soda reacts with the acid in vinegar to make carbon dioxide gas. Ask an adult to help you set up a small candle in a sand tray and mix the ingredients in a large beaker. As the mixture froths, hold the beaker above the flame. **DON'T** pour the liquid on the flame, just let the gas flow over the flame.

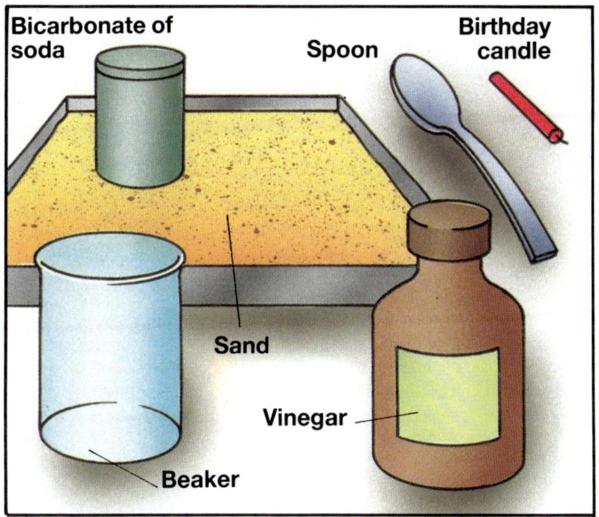

Place a birthday candle in the centre of a tray of sand

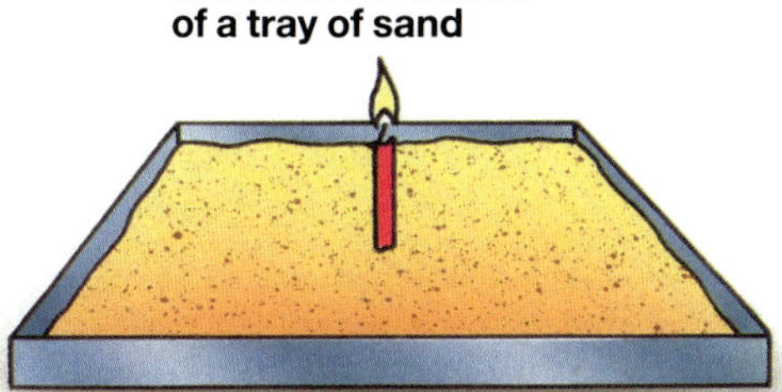

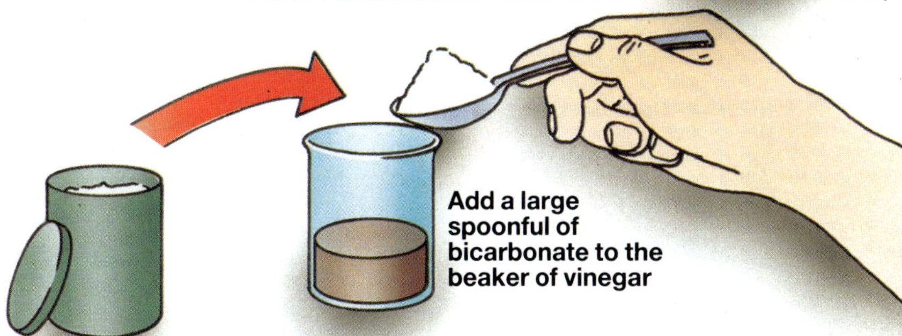

You can't see carbon dioxide gas, but because it is heavier than air it pours over the candle flame and smothers it.

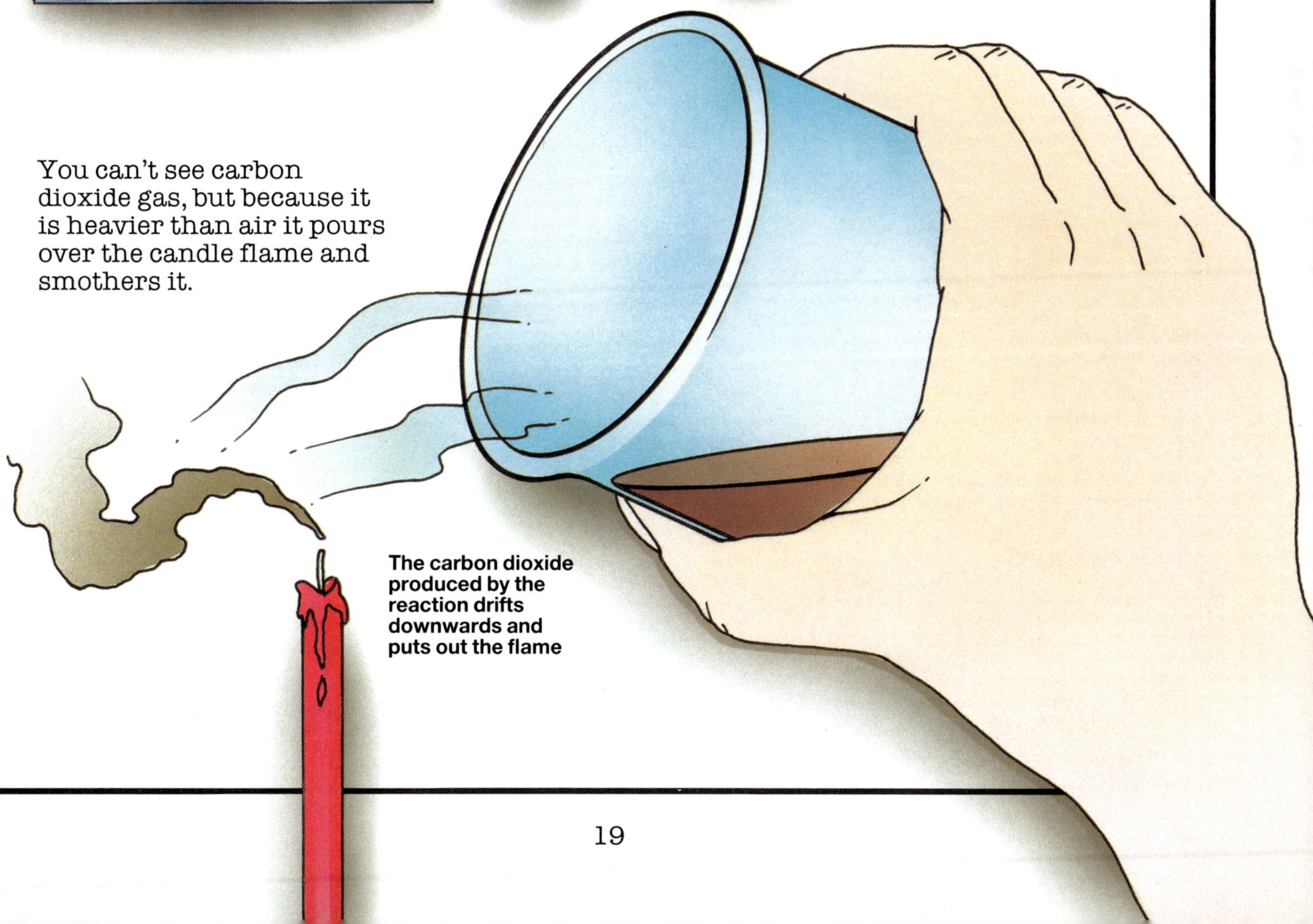

GROWING FOOD

Compare the effects of growing seeds under different conditions. Use fast-growing seeds, such as cress, and prepare your samples in exactly the same way. Line the trays with a pad of cotton wool and soak it with the same amount of water, so that it is very damp but not running with excess water. Sprinkle the same quantity of seeds evenly over the cotton wool. Keep one in a warm, sunny position – this is called the control sample. Place a second sample in the same place, but cover the tray with a lid that does not let in light. When the cress in the first tray is growing well, compare the growth with the second sample. What differences do you notice?

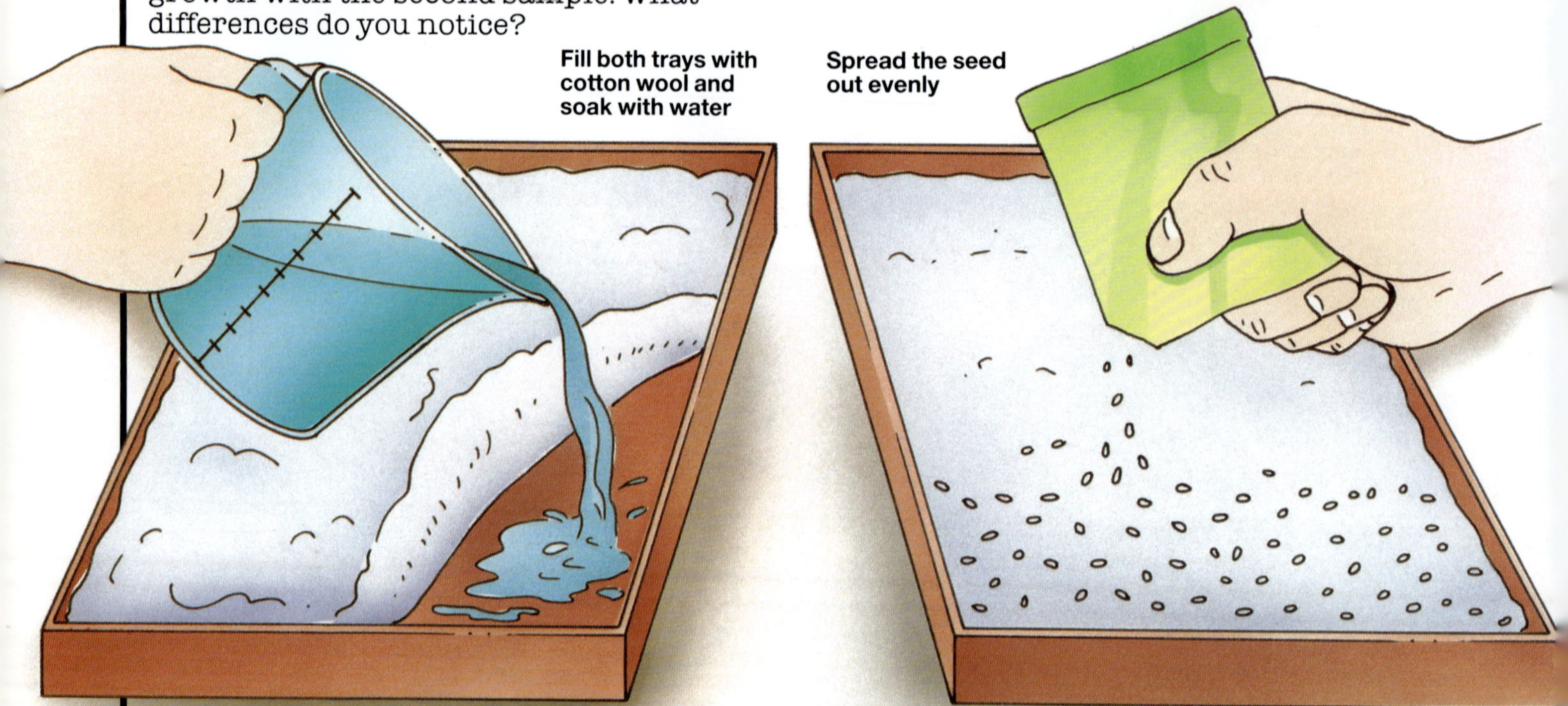

With other samples you can test the effect of pollution on plant growth. Grow one sample using pure water and place it in a warm, sunny position as before. Make up a second tray, but ask an adult to soak the cotton wool in water containing two tablespoons full of bleach. Add a similar amount of washing-up liquid to a third sample. Compare the growth and appearance of the cress plants. What differences do you notice?

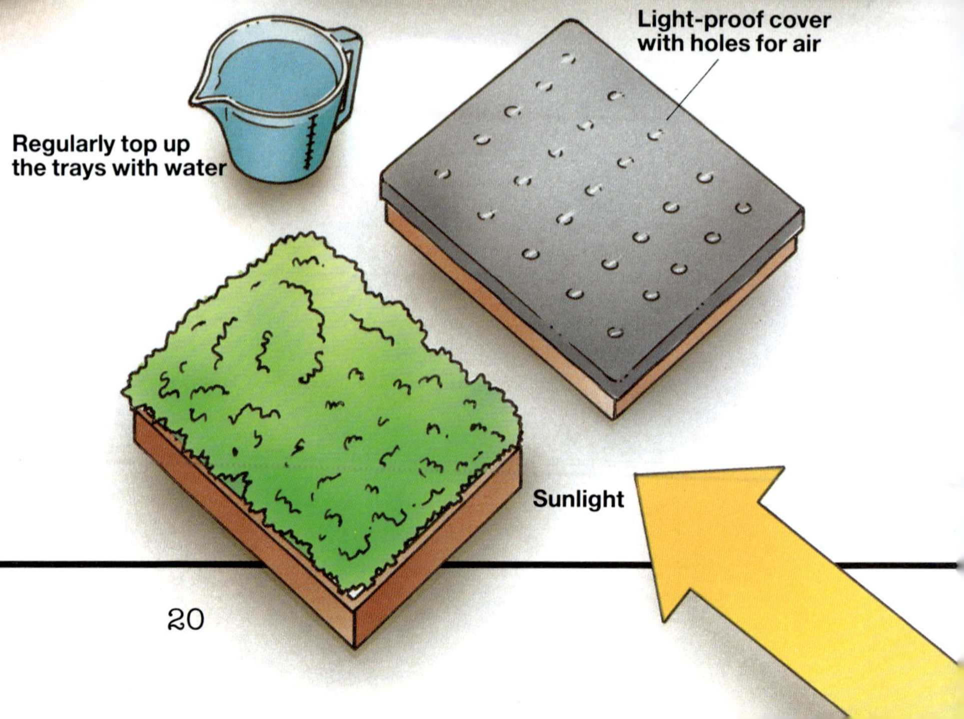

ROTTING

Find several glass, screw-topped jars and place a different sample of food or even some milk into each one. Screw on the lids and seal with sticky tape. Watch the changes that take place over a few weeks. Bacteria in the food causes decay. Because the substances that form may be dangerous, **DO NOT OPEN** the jars. Dispose of them carefully.

RUSTING

Some metals that are left unprotected may begin to rust. Use samples of steel wool or clean iron nails or even dressmakers' pins to see why this happens. Leave one piece of steel wool or some nails or pins in a plastic dish with a little water. Keep the sample damp. In another dish completely cover the wool or nails in water from a kettle that has boiled and then gone cold. Leave a third sample in a dry dish in a warm dry spot. What do you predict will happen to your metal samples?

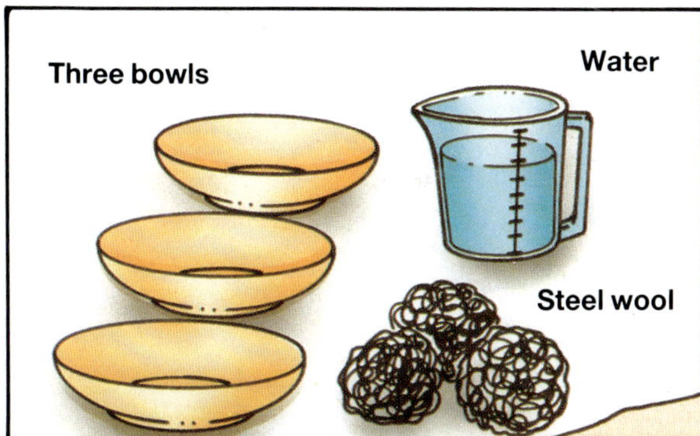

To rust, metals need moisture and oxygen. Boiled water has no air, so the sample may not rust. Samples kept damp and open to the air will rust quickly.

PHYSICS OF HEAT

Heat is a form of energy. Atoms and molecules, the tiny particles that make up everything that exists, are constantly moving and the amount of heat within any substance depends on how much and how fast its atoms move. When more heat energy is given to something its temperature rises, it expands (becomes larger) and it may change from a solid to a liquid or from a liquid to a gas. Heat can be transferred from one place to another in three ways, conduction, convection or radiation, but it can only move from a hotter area to one that has a lower temperature.

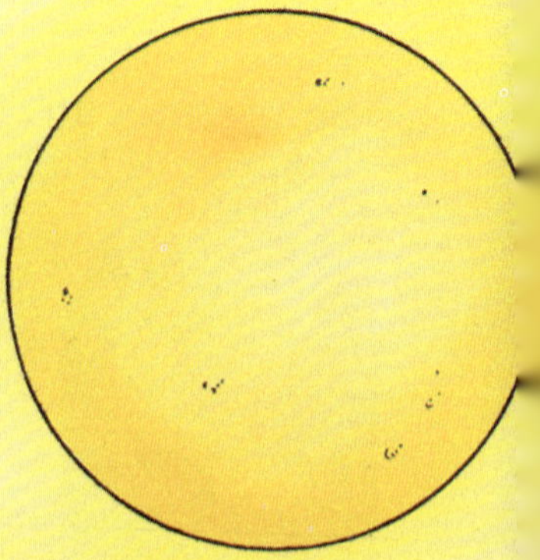

Convection
Hot air rises. The air over a fire, or over an area heated by the Sun, gets hotter and rises, letting colder air flow in below it. Heated water also rises and cooler water flows in to form swirling currents.

Radiation
Nearly all our heat and light come from the Sun. The Sun is 150 million kilometres away, but its heat and light radiation pass through space and reach us at the speed of light eight minutes later.

Conduction
Heat moves through solid objects by conduction. Put a metal spoon in a hot drink and the handle gets warm. The heat around the spoon warms the metal and passes through it along the handle. Some things, like metals, are good heat conductors. Others, called insulators, are not.

PRINCIPLES OF TEMPERATURE

How hot is hot?
Get three bowls with water at different temperatures. Put one hand into a bowl of hot water and the other into cold water. After half a minute put both hands into a bowl of warm water. This water should feel the same to both hands but it doesn't. The cold hand thinks it is in hot water, the hot hand thinks it is in cold water.

Calibration
Measuring temperatures by touch would mean many mistakes, so we need a standard measure. Liquids, like alcohol and mercury, expand when heated. A thin tube filled with one of these liquids reacts to temperature changes. The tube can be marked at points showing where the liquid expands to when it is heated, and where it contracts to when cooled. The standard temperature points are fixed at the freezing point and boiling point of pure water. The thermometer tube can then be marked at intervals between these fixed points so that it can be used to measure temperatures accurately. Marking a thermometer in this way is called calibration.

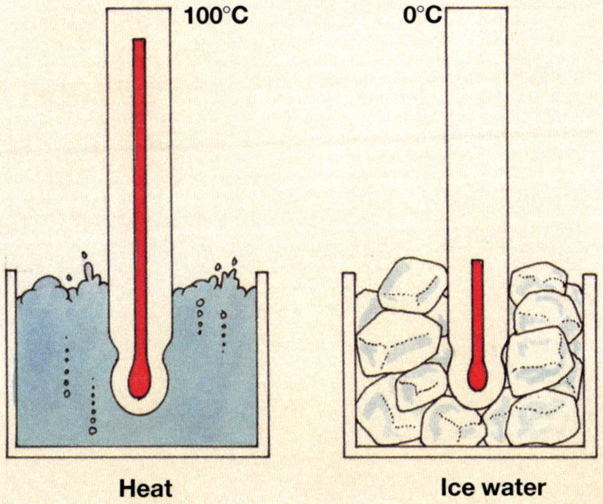

Temperature scales
There are three temperature scales commonly used today. Gabriel Fahrenheit of Germany fixed the freezing point at 32°F and boiling point at 212°F. Anders Celsius of Sweden devised the Celsius scale with 0°C as the freezing point and 100°C as the boiling point. Later a British scientist, William Kelvin, gave us the idea of an absolute zero, the lowest possible temperature, which sets the freezing point of water at 273°K and the boiling point at 373°K. Because it is confusing to have three different scales, the one used most often is the Celsius scale, although many people still use Fahrenheit to describe the weather.

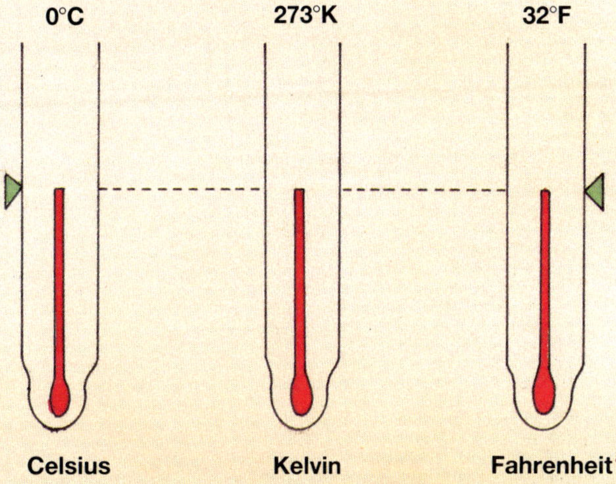

KEEPING WARM

Find four jars with lids and ask an adult to pour hot water of the same temperature into each one. Replace the lids, wrap one jar in a handkerchief, another in a thick woollen scarf and put a third in a box of polystyrene chips or sawdust. Don't wrap the fourth jar. Record the temperature in each jar with a thermometer every half an hour. Which one stays warmest and which one cools fastest?

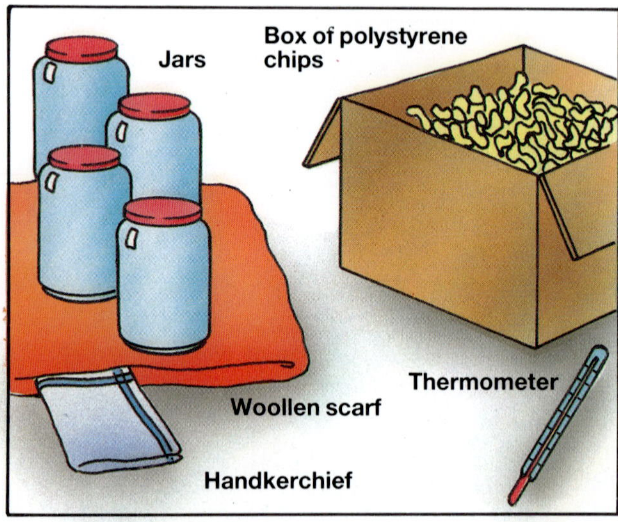

A well wrapped (insulated) jar keeps its heat best. Use this test to compare all kinds of materials to find the best insulators.

Thermos flask
A thermos flask has a sealed double-walled glass container with a vacuum inside. Heat cannot be conducted or convected through a vacuum. Radiated heat is reflected back in by the silvered glass that acts like a mirror. The only heat loss is through the cap, which is well insulated, so hot liquids stay hot for a long time.

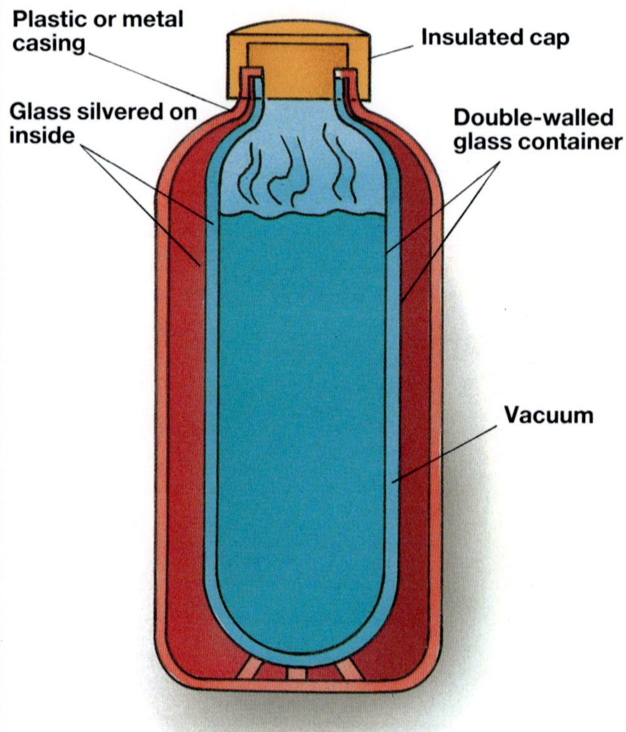

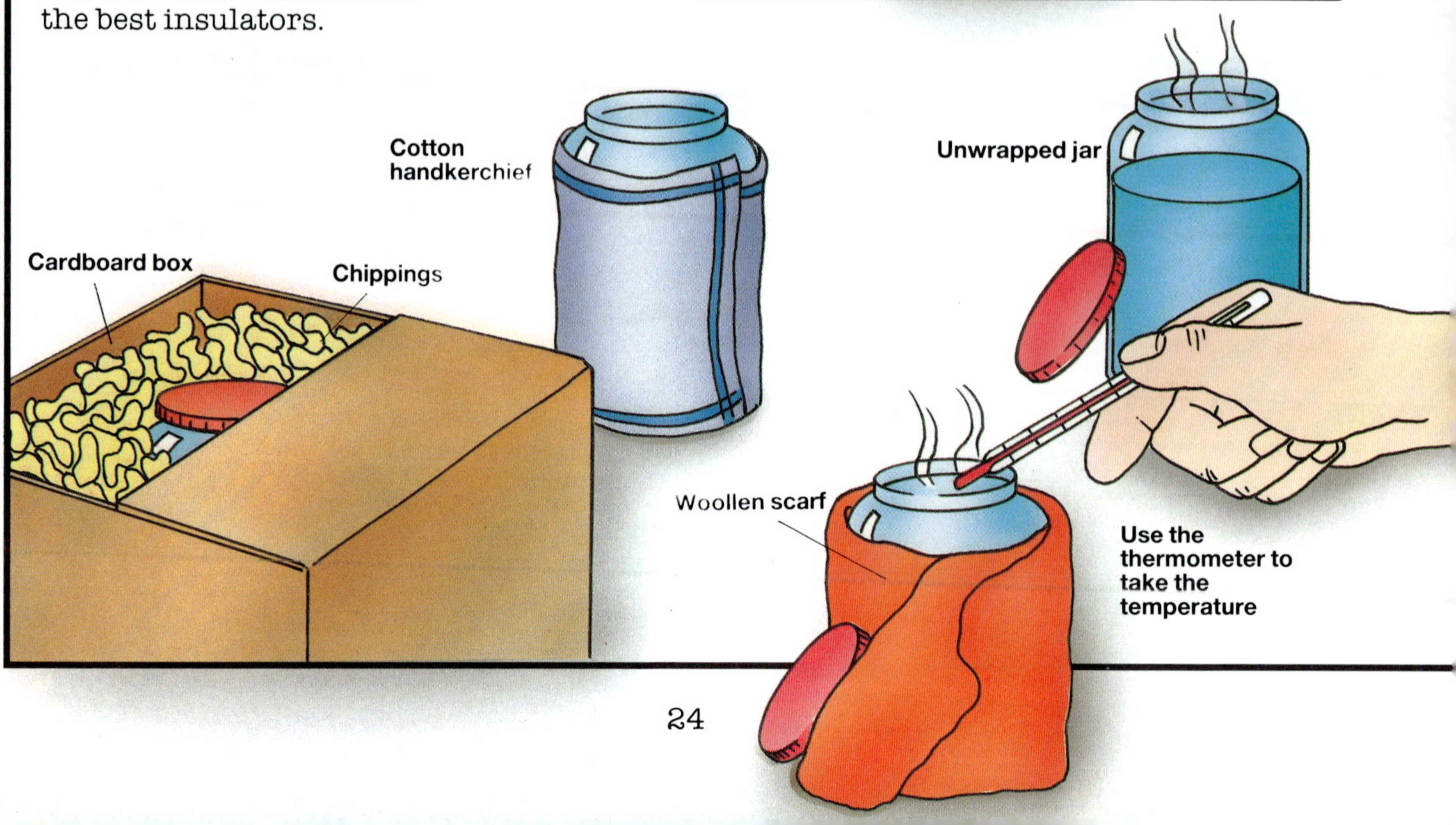

RAISING YOUR CAP

Water is at its most dense, the point where it takes up the smallest amount of space, at a temperature of 4°C. As water freezes into ice it actually expands. This is why water pipes can burst in the winter. Fill a plastic bottle to the very top with cold water. Cover the top with a foil cap and place the bottle upright in a freezer. Leave overnight, then see what has happened. As the water freezes it can only go up.

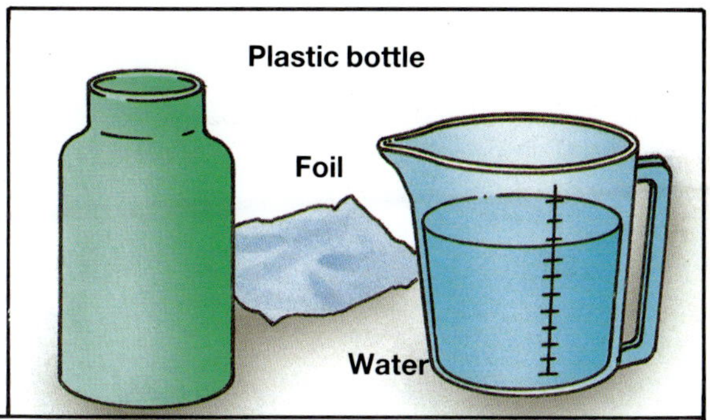

PUDDLE WATCHING

After a period of heavy rain, find a large puddle and scratch around its edge with a sharp stone, or mark it with chalk. Leave the puddle for about 15 minutes and do the same again. Repeat this four or five times. What do you notice about the puddle? The water seems to be disappearing. But where is it going? Can you estimate how much water disappears during each 15-minute period?

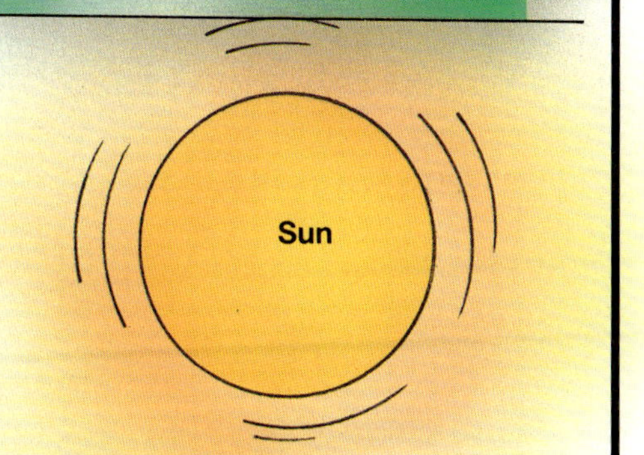

What is happening is that heat from the Sun, helped by wind, makes the water evaporate. You cannot see water vapour in the air, but it is carried into the atmosphere, forming clouds.

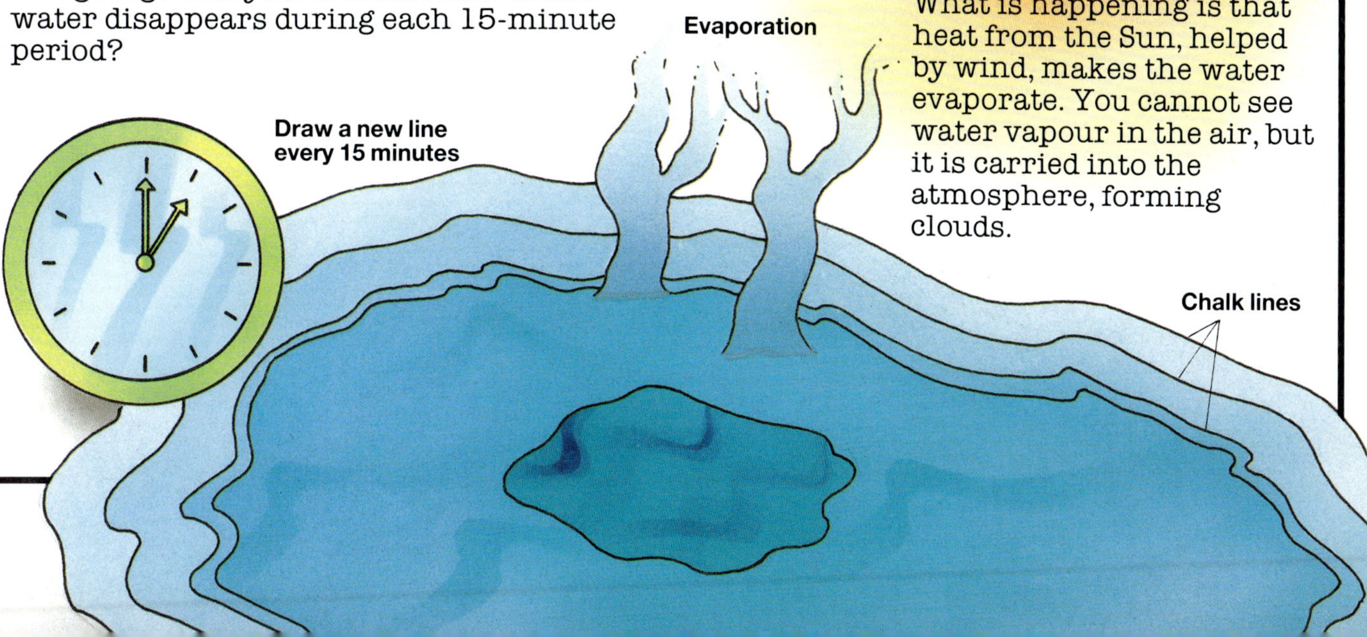

CONVECTION CURRENTS

Put a few drops of ink or food dye in a bottle and fill it with hot water. Cover the top with a foil cap with some thread attached. Lower the bottle into a tank full of clear, cold water. Let the water settle, then pull the foil away, using the thread. Watch as the hot coloured water rises in the tank and swirls around, following the convection currents of cold water flowing in towards the bottle.

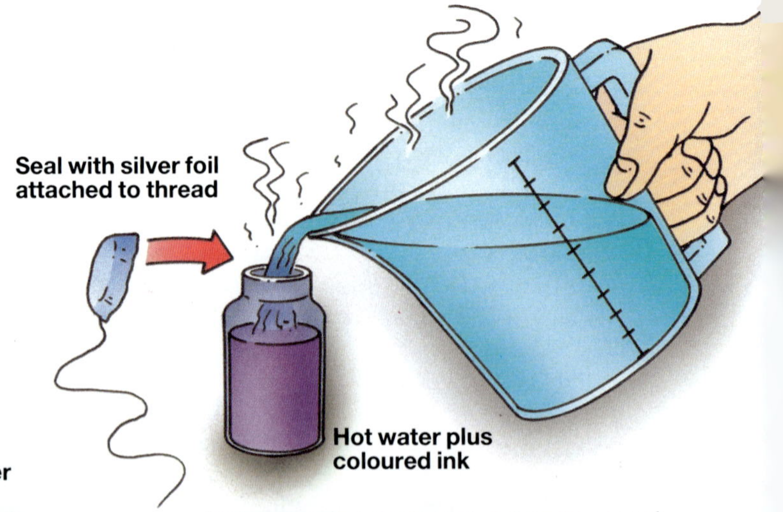

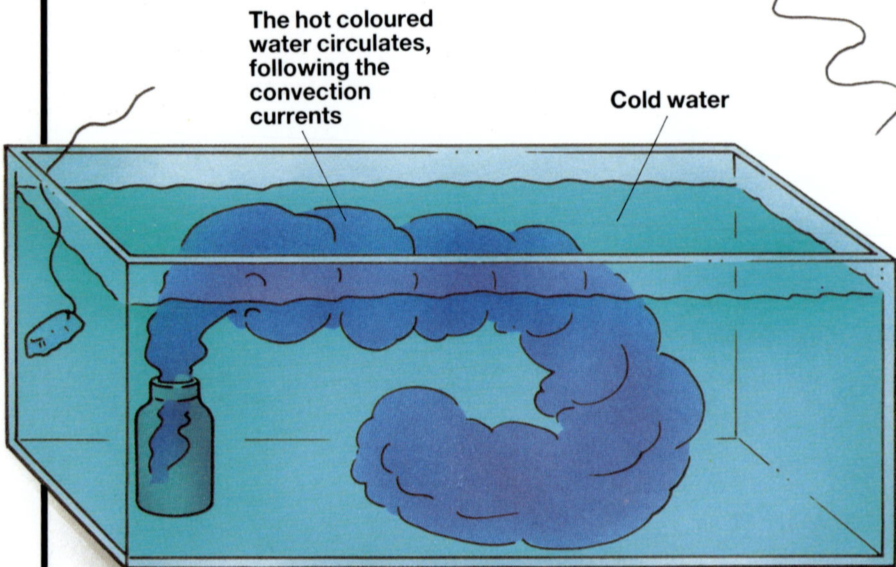

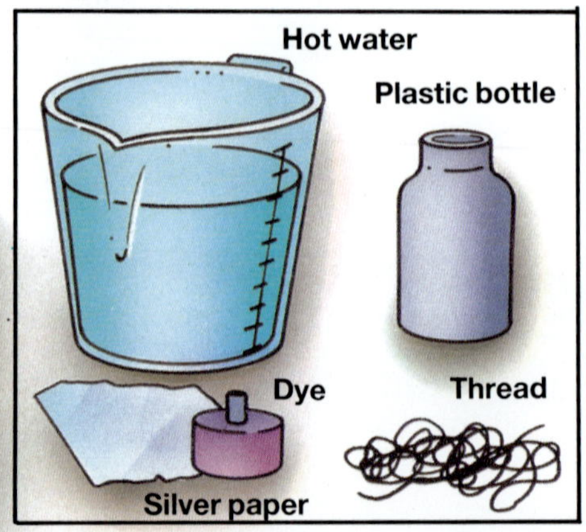

HEAT CONDUCTORS

You can watch the speed with which heat is conducted along a solid object by using candle wax. Ask an adult to help you drip candle wax onto a long nail. Hold the nail with a clothes peg or pair of pliers. Put the end of the nail in a candle flame. As the heat is conducted along the nail the wax begins to melt and drip off.

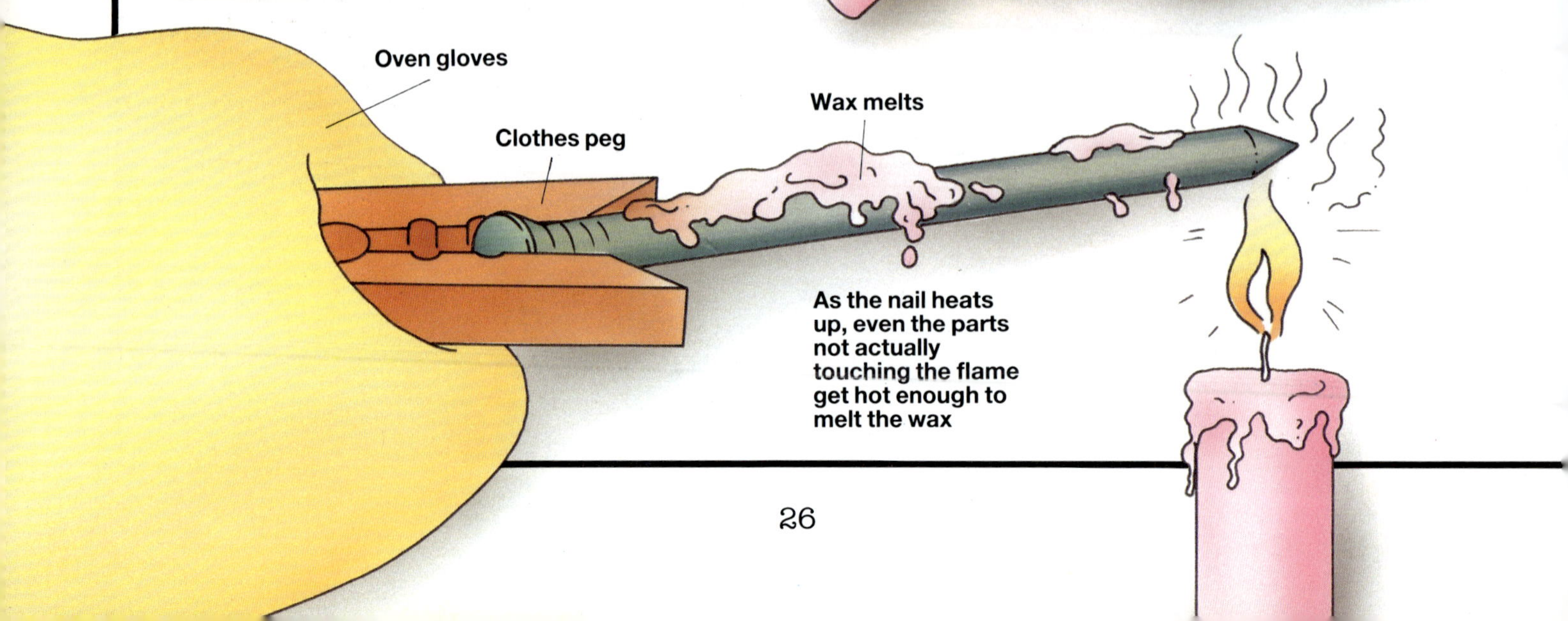

SPIRAL SNAKE

Carefully cut a circle from a sheet of thin paper and cut it into a spiral shape. Hang the spiral from a length of thread over a hot central heating radiator or storage heater. **DO NOT** hang it over a fire or flame. The rising hot air currents catch the spiral, making it twist and turn. In a room, the convection currents that form around a radiator or fire carry the heat all round the room, so that eventually every corner of the room is warmed.

RADIATED HEAT

Radiated heat can be reflected away. Take two identical glass jars, filled with the same amount of cold water. Cover one in black paper and the other in silver foil, then put them in a sunny place for about an hour. Check the temperature. What do you find?

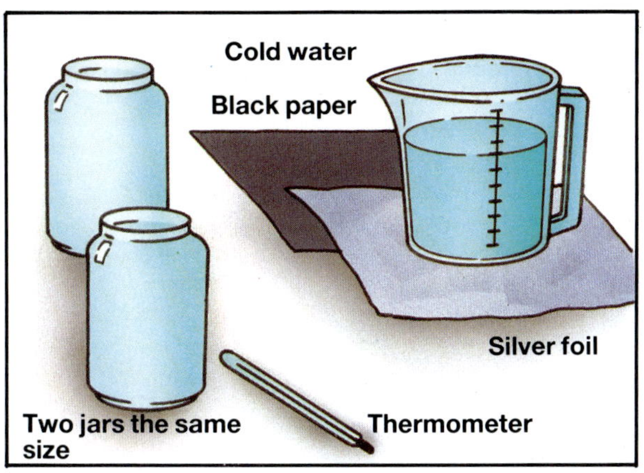

SOURCES OF ENERGY

All of our energy comes from the Sun, whether it is direct heat and light from the Sun's radiated energy, or stored chemical energy in fuels and food. Our problem is that our demand for energy increases every day. Everything in our lives depends on the constant supply of power, particularly electrical power. Think of all the things you use that need electricity to work. Almost every industry needs electrical energy. We use vast quantities of energy. Without it, life as we know it could not continue. So where can all this energy come from?

Gas, coal and oil
We think of fuels as gas, coal and oil. Coal has been important for hundreds of years and oil provides us with petrol and plastics that are in increasing demand. What can we do when these fuels run out?

Wind and water
Waves build up energy as they move across oceans and wind can be powerful enough to uproot trees. Engineers are investigating many interesting ways to harness this natural power, including wave-driven turbines and wind generators.

Nuclear power
Scientists discovered that elements such as uranium and plutonium can be used as a source of nuclear energy, giving out vast quantities of heat that could be used destructively in bombs or as a controlled source of energy in nuclear power stations.

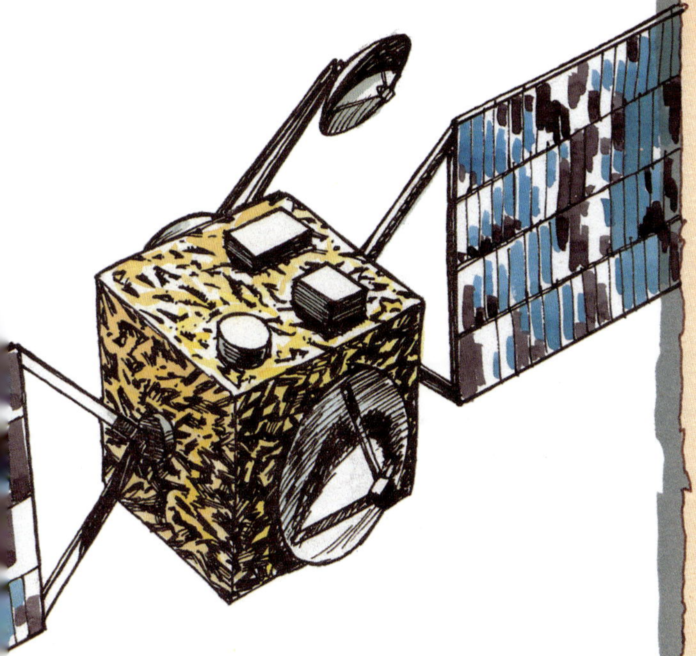

Solar power
In many hot countries, solar panels are used to capture the Sun's heat energy. Water is pumped through a series of pipes laid under a glass panel which is heated by the Sun, giving cheap hot water.

PRINCIPLES OF SUPPLY

Fossil fuels
Fossil fuels were made over millions of years by the action of pressure and heat upon layers of dead plant and animal tissue under the ground and the sea. Because this process takes so much time, and because we use so much of these fuels to make electricity, Earth's reserves of fossil fuels have almost gone, so we need to develop other sources of power.

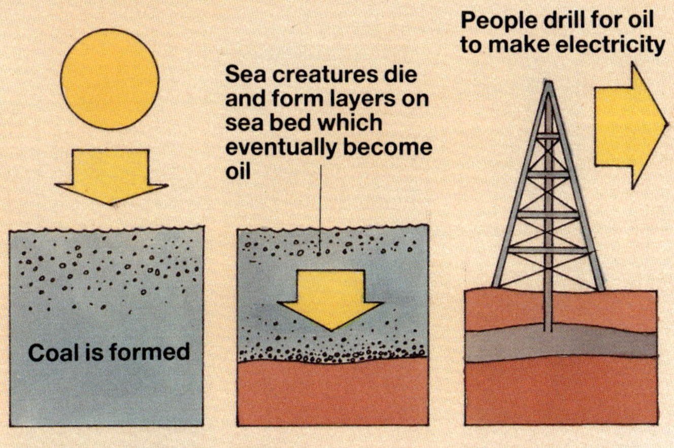

Renewable power
Wind always blows and water constantly flows, providing a free, continuous source of energy. We need to find ways to use this. One that has been used for many years is hydro-electricity. Water trapped behind a dam is released and rushes over turbines, turning them very fast. The turbines are connected to generators that produce electricity.

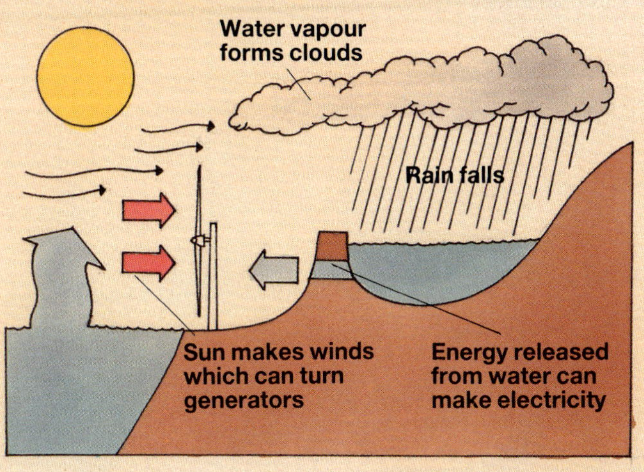

MAKE YOUR OWN WINDMILL

Modern windmills have two or three blades that are specially shaped like an aircraft's wing (an aerofoil shape) to catch the wind and turn at the highest possible speed. The energy that is produced when the blades turn is used to turn a generator that makes electricity. A large wind generator can produce a great deal of electrical power. The windmill shown here turns a little acrobat figure attached to a crank on the windmill blades. Follow the step by step instructions to set your acrobat tumbling.

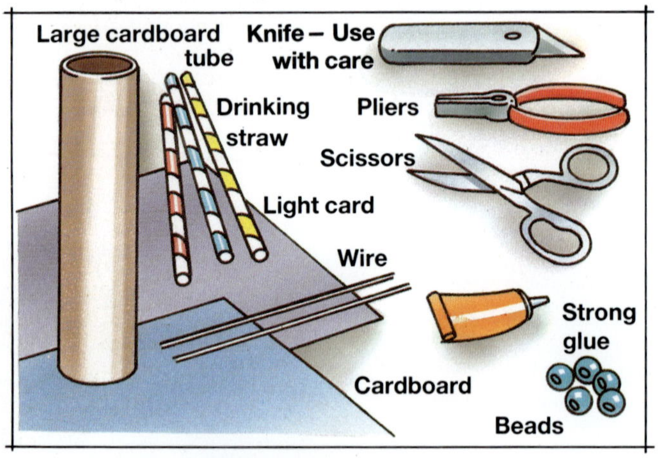

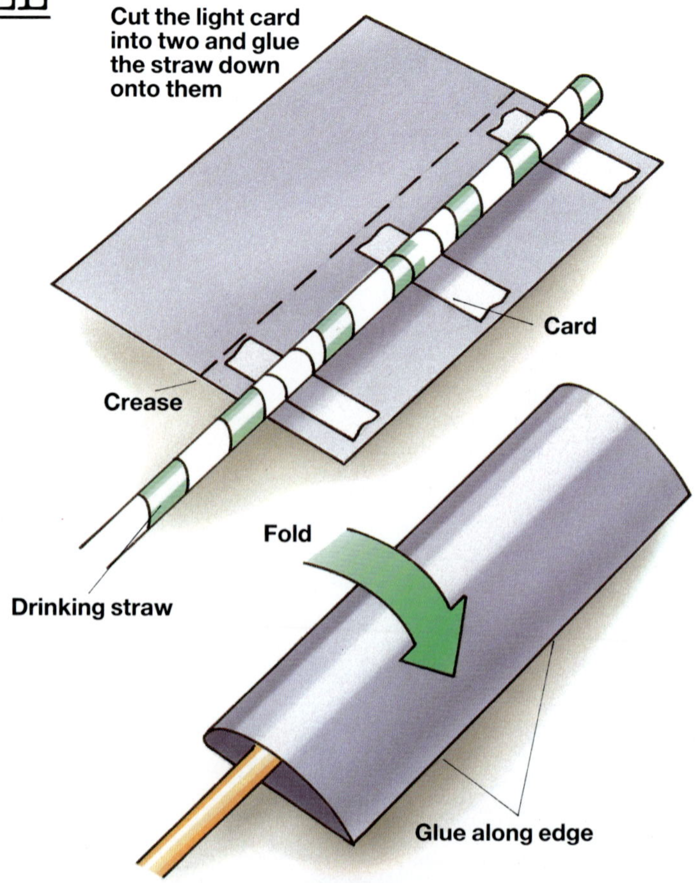

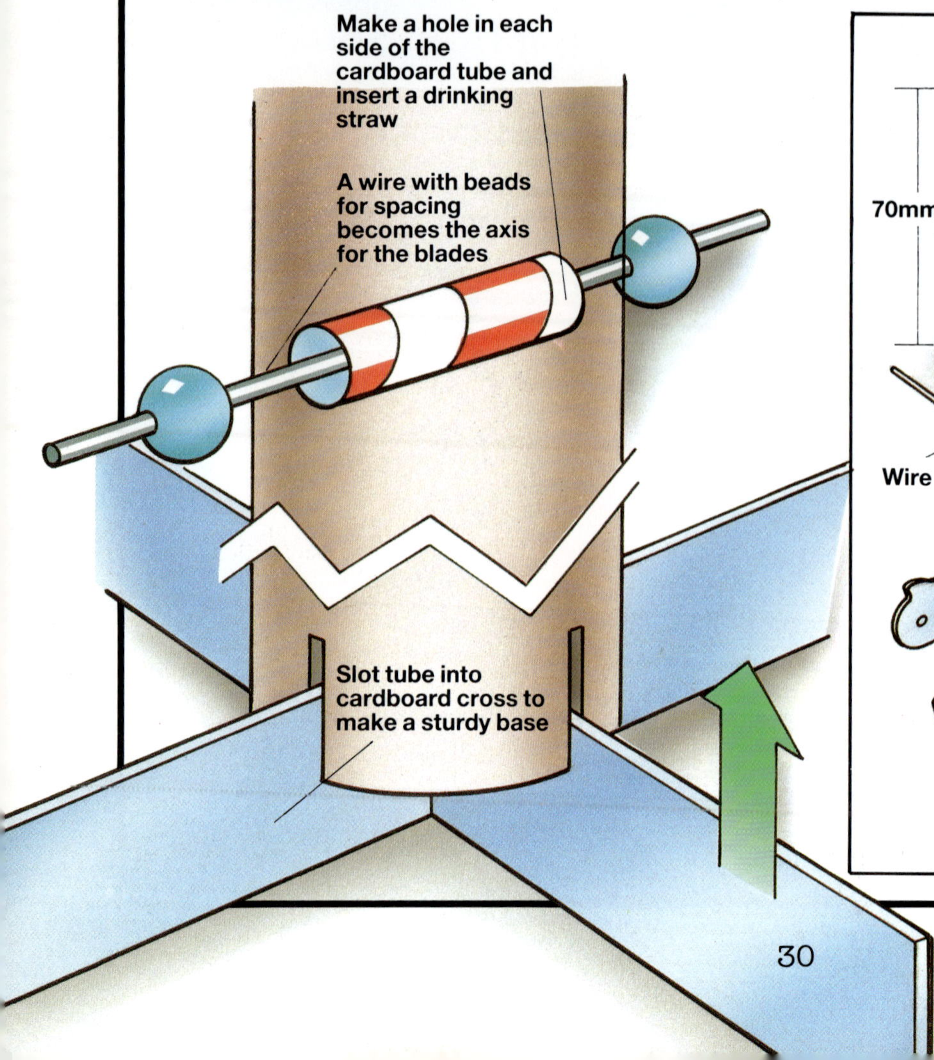

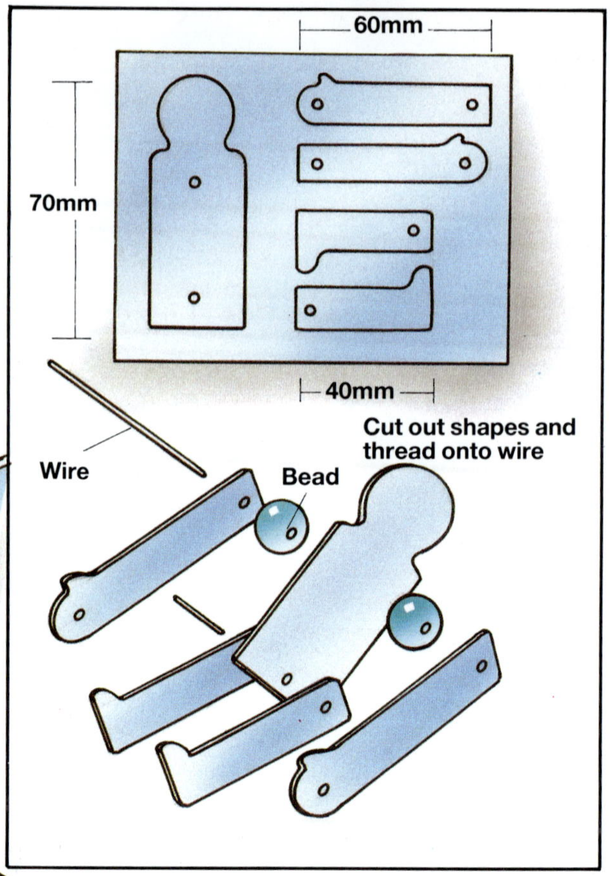

FUTURE ENERGY

Burning fossil fuels can damage our environment by releasing harmful gases. Carbon dioxide released from burning fuels forms a layer in the atmosphere that causes global warming. We need to get more energy from the Sun, wind and waves. We also need to save energy by recycling household waste like glass, metals and paper.

Solar energy

Wave power

Wind power

Geothermal energy

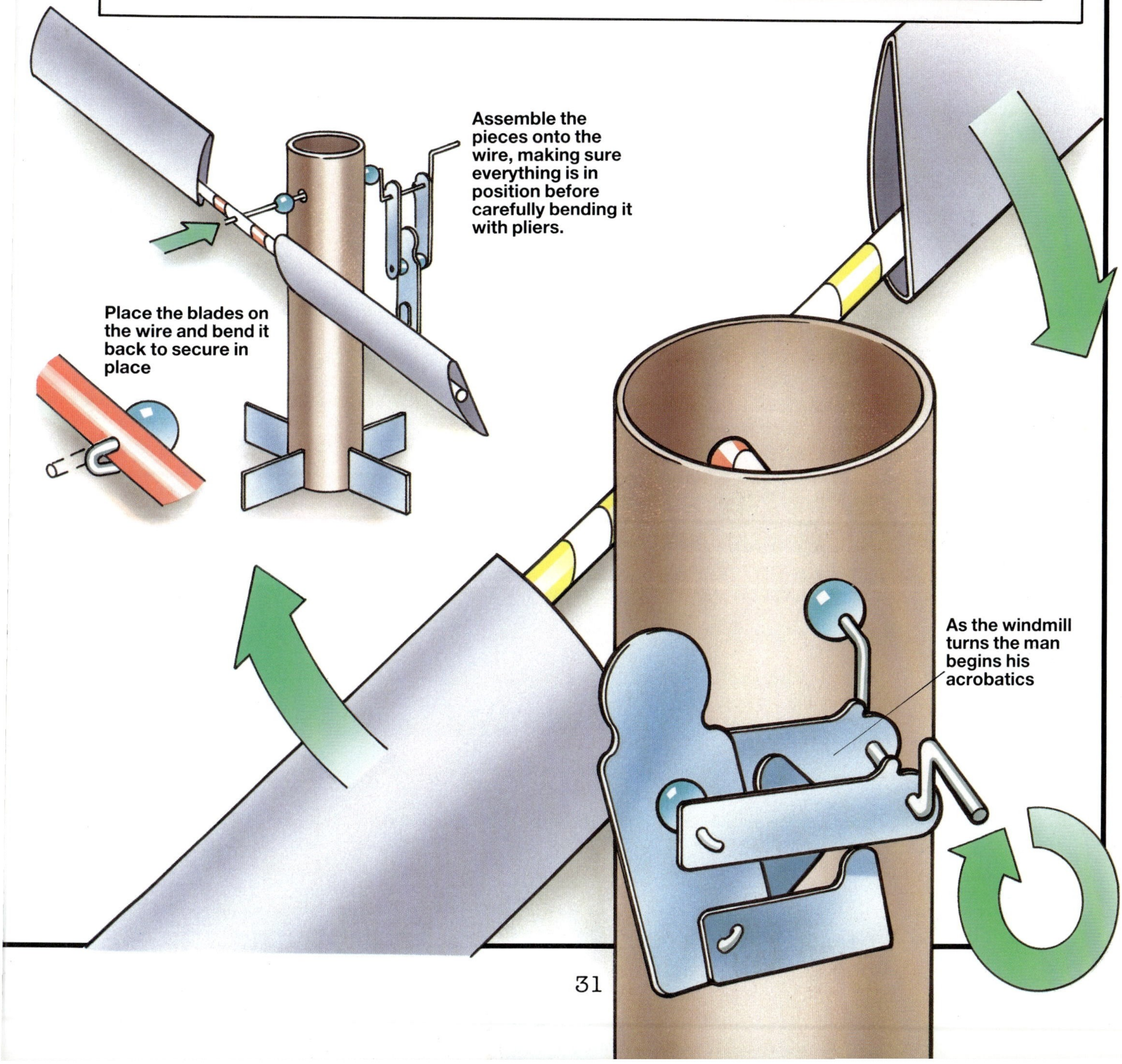

NUCLEAR FISSION

Everything is made from tiny particles called atoms. Some atoms are so large they are unstable and cannot hold together. They break up, giving out a burst of energy and releasing nuclear particles called neutrons. In a large mass of unstable atoms these "free" neutrons can make more atoms break up, creating a continuous reaction called nuclear fission. Early this century it was discovered that some substances like uranium could be made to break up in this way, giving out heat energy that can be used to make electricity. The problem is that this reaction is very dangerous and has to be very carefully controlled. It also leaves large amounts of deadly radioactive waste to be disposed of.

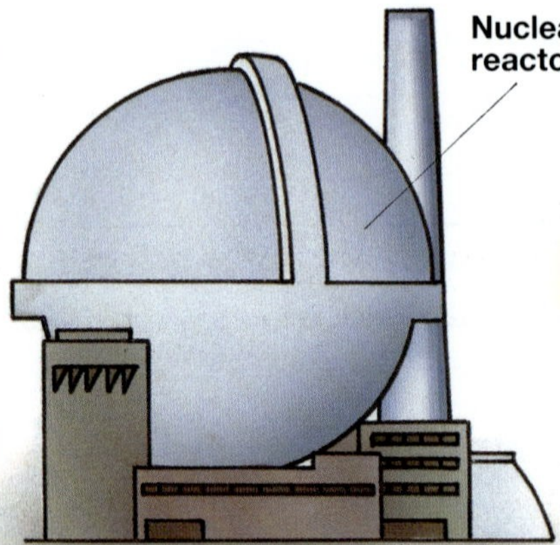

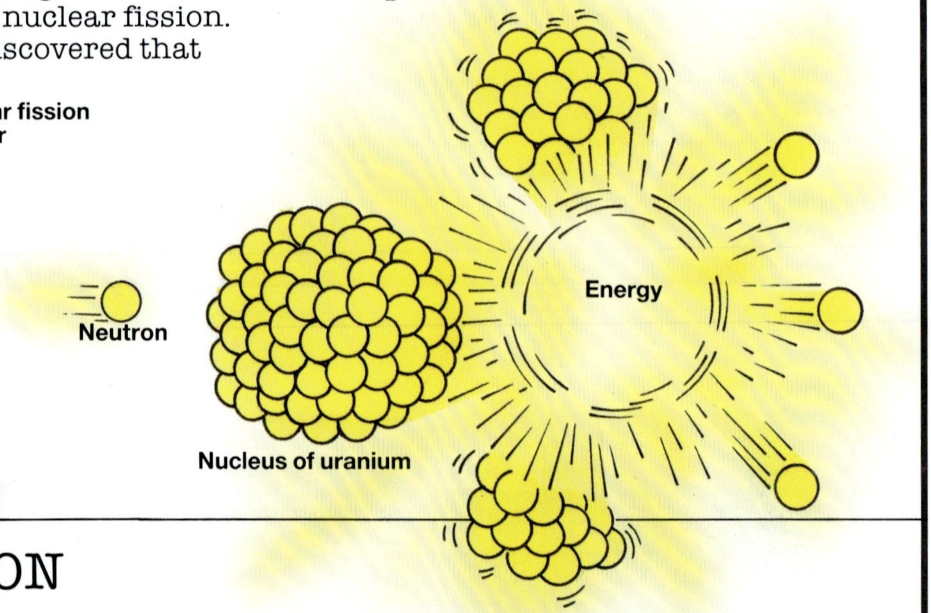

NUCLEAR FUSION

The Sun's energy comes from a process called nuclear fusion. Under very strong heat and pressure, special hydrogen atoms, called deuterium and tritium, combine together to form helium. As this happens, tremendous amounts of heat and light energy are produced. This principle has been used to make nuclear fusion weapons (often called hydrogen bombs) that have terrifying destructive power. Scientists all over the world are trying to find a way to control fusion reactions here on Earth. If they succeed, the energy produced will last us almost for ever. Also, it will not bring any of the current problems that we have with waste polluting the environment, just cheap energy for everyone.

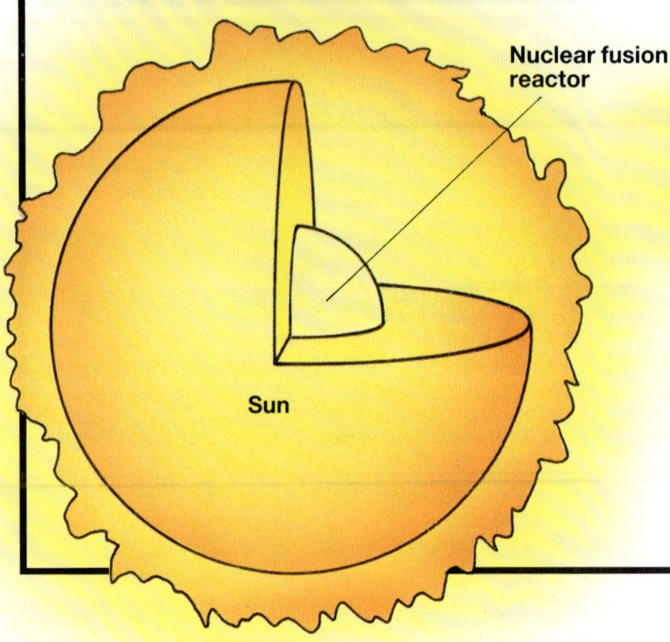

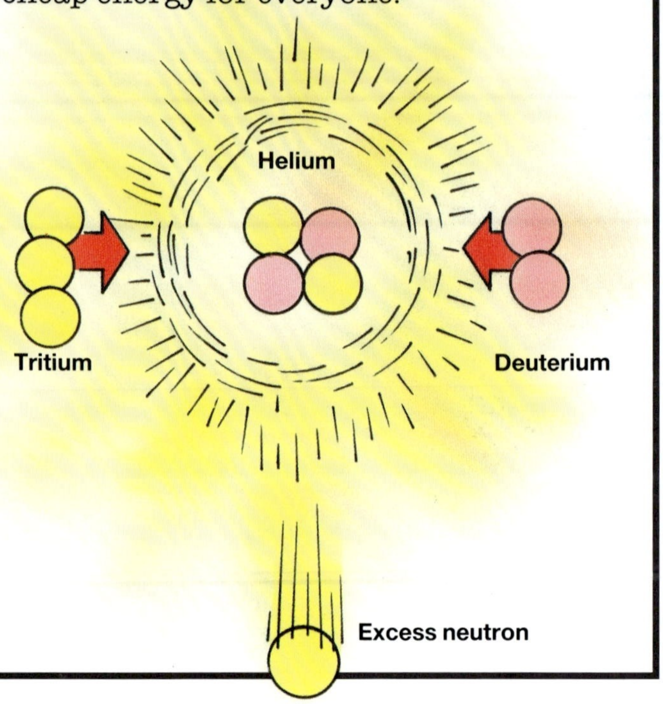